Edgar Allan Poe

Edgar Allan Poe

A BIOGRAPHY

Twenty-First Century Books ✥ Brookfield, Connecticut

Cover photography courtesy of Maryland Historical Society
Photographs courtesy of Rare Book & Manuscript Library, Columbia University: p. 2;
Getty Images/Hulton/Archive: pp. 8, 53, 60; Brown Brothers: pp. 13, 41, 49, 55, 70, 131;
Harvard Theatre Collection, The Houghton Library: p. 15; Collection of the New-York
Historical Society: pp. 16, 76, 101; Maryland Department, Enoch Pratt Free Library:
p. 21; Edgar Allan Poe Museum: pp. 22 (both), 63, 86; Valentine Richmond History
Center: p. 31; The Lilly Library, Indiana University, Bloomington, Indiana: p. 33; Special
Collections, Alderman Library, University of Virginia, Charlottesville: p. 34; Print and
Picture Collection, Free Library of Philadelphia: pp. 83, 109; Drexel University Archives
(W. W. Hagerty Library, 33rd & Market Streets, Philadelphia, PA 19104-2875): p. 85
(Poe, Edgar Allan. "The murders in the Rue Morgue: Facsimile of the ms in the Drexel
Institute." Philadelphia: George Barrie & Sons, [1895]. p. 5); © Bettmann/Corbis:
p. 93; Private Collection/Bridgeman Art Library: p. 95; © Museum of the City
of New York: p. 99; © American Antiquarian Society: p. 103; The Bronx County
Historical Society Collection: p. 119; New York Public Library: p. 123;
Library of Congress: p. 127 (#LC-USZ62-104482)

Library of Congress Cataloging-in-Publication Data
Meltzer, Milton, 1915–
Edgar Allan Poe : a biography / by Milton Meltzer.
p. cm.
Summary: Examines the troubled life of the nineteenth-century writer
whose poetry and short stories broke new ground in American literature.
Includes bibliographical references (p.) and index.
ISBN 0-7613-2910-2 (lib. bdg.)
1. Poe, Edgar Allan, 1809–1849—Juvenile literature. 2. Authors,
American—19th century—Biography—Juvenile literature. [1. Poe, Edgar
Allan, 1809–1849. 2. Authors, American.] I. Title.
PS2631 .M45 2003
818'.309—dc21 2002155802

Published by Twenty-First Century Books
A Division of The Millbrook Press, Inc.
2 Old New Milford Road
Brookfield, Connecticut 06804
www.millbrookpress.com

Printed in the United States of America

2 4 5 3 1

Also by Milton Meltzer

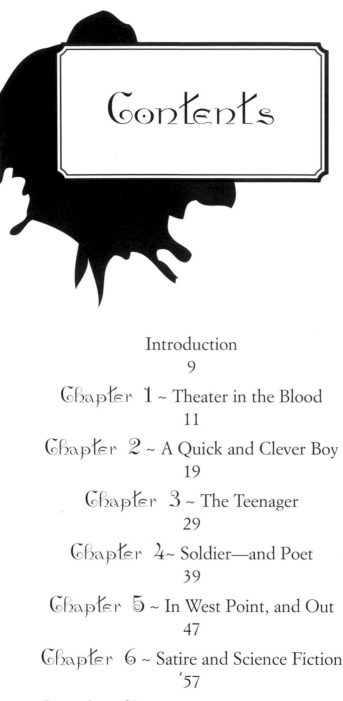

Contents

AN ARTIST'S RESPONSE TO "THE RAVEN"

Introduction

Once upon a midnight dreary, while I pondered, weak and weary . . .

It begins with that line, a poem that millions of boys and girls have read, recited, and often memorized while in school.

"The Raven" is one of the best-known poems in literature. Its popularity is worldwide. Edgar Allan Poe wrote it in 1845, and it has been in print ever since. Poe's verse, says the scholar Harold Bloom, "must have a larger audience than any other American poet, including Whitman and Frost."

But Poe is valued not only for his poetry. He was also a prolific writer of short stories, the creator of two literary forms that readers everywhere enjoy—the detective story and the horror thriller. Countless fans have enjoyed the products of his invention in magazines, in books, on TV series, and in the movies.

Poe's life was short, and painful. Who he was, what he sprang from, why and how he wrote, as well as the troubled life he led as one of the first American writers to try to make a living solely by their pen, will be explored in these chapters.

1

Theater in the Blood

THEATER WAS IN EDGAR ALLAN POE'S BLOOD.
As he grew up, people would say later, he often behaved as
though he were performing dramatic roles to please or to shock
an audience. The desire to perform was solidly grounded in his
parentage. His mother, born Eliza Arnold in England, was herself the child of Elizabeth Arnold, an actress known on the
London stage. When her first husband died, Elizabeth took her
little girl, Eliza, to America. They arrived in 1796, soon after the
American colonists had broken free of Britain to create their
democratic republic.

Eliza's widowed mother, about twenty-four, married a musi-
cian, and together they joined a troupe of actors, traveling to perform anywhere an audience could be found. Only nine years old,
Eliza made her stage debut in Boston, in a production that fea-
tured her mother. The critics praised the child for her beauty, her
innocence, and her talent, so startling in one so young. Two years
later, Eliza's mother died, possibly of yellow fever.

In an extraordinary career, Eliza would play nearly three
hundred roles, from trashy farce to high-quality comedy and
tragedy, including Shakespeare's Juliet, Ophelia, and Cordelia.

MINIATURE PORTRAIT OF POE'S MOTHER, ELIZA

At fifteen, she married a teenaged actor, who died only a few years later. At nineteen, Eliza married again, this time a young Baltimore law student, David Poe Jr. He enjoyed playing in amateur productions, saw Eliza on stage, fell in love, and quit the law to join her theater company.

Their first child, Henry Poe, was born in 1807, and at the age of two was placed in the care of friends in Baltimore while his parents toured.

David Poe, a handsome man three years older than Eliza, was often cast as a romantic hero. In six years he played over a hundred roles. Unfortunately he was rated by the critics as nowhere near as talented as his wife, Eliza. With a hair-trigger temper David often quarreled with his wife and threatened critics whose mocking reviews he took as insults.

Theater companies were almost always on the road in those days, giving performances in town and cities all along the East Coast. To survive in a poorly paid and poorly esteemed profession, actors had to perform anywhere, at anytime, and as often as possible. Eliza especially enjoyed playing in Boston, where she had made her debut as a nine-year-old. For three years she and David made the city the heart of their whirligig theatrical life.

During their third year in Boston the couple's second son, Edgar, was born in a cheap rooming house near the Boston Common, on January 19, 1809.

Eliza had performed on the Boston stage until one week before the birth. And one month after, she was back on the stage. What to do with the baby? Who would care for him? Where would Eliza and David get the extra money needed now? David couldn't turn to his father, who had severely disapproved of his son marrying an actress and quitting the law. Frantic, feeling helpless, he began to drink more and more.

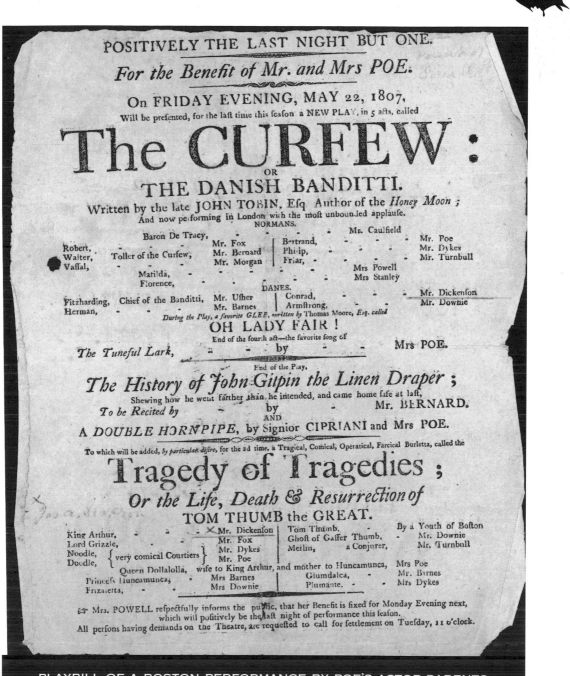

PLAYBILL OF A BOSTON PERFORMANCE BY POE'S ACTOR-PARENTS

Edgar
Allan
Poe

POE AT THE AGE OF FIVE

Five weeks later, the Poes left their baby in Baltimore with his paternal grandparents, and went back on the road. That would be the pattern when Edgar's sister, Rosalie, was born (1810) and the children would be moved here, there, and everywhere. While Edgar was still an infant, David Poe deserted his wife and children. They never saw him again. His drinking had gone so far that he was even drunk on stage. Perhaps he was fired by the company manager. Toward the end of 1811, it appears that David died—probably of tuberculosis, or TB—in Norfolk, Virginia.

Eliza Poe, only twenty-four, died that same December. She gave her last performance in Richmond, Virginia, on October 11, 1811, already quite sick of what was then called consumption, and was later recognized as tuberculosis, a disease commonly of the lungs, caused by the tubercle bacillus. More died of it than of any other cause, for its cure would not be discovered for another hundred years and more.

The hard life on tour, the unending poverty, the desertion of her husband, the agonizing concern for her children's fate—all may have become too much for Eliza to endure.

And Edgar? What would become of a little child left without mother, father, or a penny?

2

A Quick and Clever Boy

DURING ELIZA'S LAST ILLNESS, EDGAR AND his sister Rosalie were cared for by Mr. and Mrs. Luke Usher, actor friends of his parents. Poe had never really known his mother and father, he said later. Yet their loss must have had a lasting effect. As tuberculosis wore away Eliza, the racking coughs, the hemorrhages, the crimsoning sheets, and the feeble, silent figure on her deathbed could not be forgotten. That he was left with the enduring memory of a lovely, dying young woman would be evidenced again and again in the images of his poems and stories.

The eldest child, Henry, was being raised by David Poe's parents in Baltimore. The Mackenzie family in Richmond adopted Rosalie Poe. And Edgar was taken into the home of John and Frances "Fanny" Allan, probably on her initiative, for she herself had been an orphan, and in a childless marriage welcomed Edgar warmly. Like Eliza, Frances Allan was slender, delicate, and often downed by sickness. The Allans raised the boy as a son, but never formally adopted him.

John Allan, son of a seafaring family in Scotland, had emigrated to America at sixteen, to work for his uncle, William

POE'S HOME IN BALTIMORE

Galt, Virginia's leading merchant. Now he was partner in the modest business of Ellis and Allan, in Richmond. The firm dealt in tobacco, feed, farm animals, and slaves. (The Allan family had three slaves serving them.)

Allan resented his uncle for having refused to give him an academic education. He took pride in being a self-made man, and insisted that others stand on their own two feet. He demanded loyalty and hard work of his employees, and would expect the same of his ward, Edgar.

Eager for acceptance into Richmond's upper class—made up of merchants, planters, and professionals—John Allan read widely in literature, placed musical instruments in his home, and in company liked to drop quotations from esteemed

POE'S FOSTER PARENTS, JOHN AND FRANCES ALLAN

authors. He owned horses, went hunting, played cards, and was generous with the best liquors. Rumors spread that he had affairs with other women, and had fathered an illegitimate child, whose expenses he paid.

John's wife, Frances, though poorly educated, was a capable homemaker, with an affectionate nature that helped three-year-old Edgar find his way in a family setting totally different from the theatrical world of his parents. He had both playmates and pets to enjoy, and prided himself on the handsome clothing that the Allans dressed him in. When summer came, the Allans took the child to such fashionable resorts as White Sulphur Springs.

At five, the Allans began his schooling with a private tutor, and then sent him to a Richmond school whose master reported he was a "charming" boy who did well. Early on, with his fine memory and musical ear, Edgar showed off for family friends by reciting passages from popular English poems. Now and then Edgar saw his sister Rosalie and heard from his older brother Henry, in Baltimore.

It was his foster parents who placed "Allan" in the middle of Poe's name. Later, due to a falling out Poe had with his foster father, he would never sign himself "Edgar Allan Poe," but only "Edgar A. Poe."

In 1815, Allan's firm decided to expand abroad and sent the junior partner, with his wife and Edgar, to open a branch office in England. It was a thirty-four-day voyage across the stormy Atlantic. Six-year-old Edgar said he was proud that he never was scared.

Upon arrival, they visited Allan's relatives in Scotland, and then took lodgings in London. In April 1816, Edgar was placed in a local boarding school, where he studied spelling, history, and geography. At nine, the boy was sent to an advanced boarding school in a village a few miles north of London. A hundred years earlier, Daniel Defoe had lived there. Edgar came to love Defoe's *Robinson Crusoe* and would learn from Defoe's use of concrete details how to make his own fantastic tales believable.

At that time, English schools relied on rote learning—the memorizing of chunks of facts, dates, and passages from classic authors. Little attention was given to what things meant. The children were not encouraged to ask questions, to think for themselves. Mathematics and science were taught, as well as Latin and French. Edgar found the school dreary, dull, and too strictly disciplined.

Long after, when Poe had become known as the school's most famous pupil, its headmaster recalled that Poe could speak French, translate any easy Latin author, and knew more about history and literature than many older boys who had been given greater advantages. He told an interviewer that Poe "was a quick and clever boy and would have been a very good boy if he had not been spoiled by his parents," meaning the Allans. "But they spoiled him," he went on, "and allowed him an extravagant amount of pocket-money, which enabled him to get into all manner of mischief. . . . He was wayward and willful."

Mr. Allan was pleased with Edgar's progress. In letters to friends in Richmond he said, "Edgar is growing wonderfully, and enjoys a good reputation, and is both able and willing to receive instruction . . . He is a very fine boy and a good scholar."

In 1820, after five years in England, the family returned home. The overseas business venture had not done well, and the firm decided to close the London office.

What was America like at that time?

The population of the United States was about 9.5 million (half the size of New York State's population in the year 2000). Virginia, with a bit over 1 million, was third in size. The black population was 1.7 million, with 90 percent and more of all blacks living in the South. (No one counted the Native Americans.)

Only a few years before Poe's birth, America had doubled in area. President Thomas Jefferson's purchase of the Louisiana Territory from France in 1803 had added a tract of 828,000 square miles (2,152,000 square kilometers) lying between the Mississippi River and the Rocky Mountains. In 1819, Spain had ceded Florida to the United States. There were now twenty-two states in the Union, eleven slave and eleven free. In November 1820, James Monroe of Virginia would be elected to a second term in the White House.

America's Industrial Revolution was just getting under way, with the first textile factories, using waterpower, opening up in Massachusetts. Those plants were turning out millions of yards of cloth per year. The workers, mostly young girls from farm families, were putting in seventy hours per week. Soon after the Allans returned home, the first railroad in America began operating. Swiftly the new form of transporting people and goods would knit the country together.

The vast new territory acquired by the Louisiana Purchase raised the explosive issue of slavery. Congress began a bitter and passionate debate over whether slavery should be extended or not into the territories. As the Allans reopened their home in Richmond, Congress adopted the Compromise of 1820. Under it, the territory of Missouri came into the Union as a slave state, and Maine as a free state. So the sectional balance of political power was maintained, at twelve states each.

The young Poe, as he entered maturity, would always side with the Southern pro-slavers. He grew up in an atmosphere of fear. Virginia, one of the largest slave states, had been panicked by slave rebellions as far back as 1663. In 1800, Gabriel Prosser, a slave coachman who felt God had called upon him to deliver his people from bondage, had gathered many of his followers to attack Richmond and kill their oppressors. But he was betrayed, captured by authorities, and publicly hanged together with thirty-five other slaves. And in 1822, two years after Edgar was back home, the carpenter Denmark Vesey, in the neighboring state of South Carolina, who had bought his freedom, would plan one of the most extensive revolts against slavery ever recorded. But he too would be betrayed, and with thirty-six other blacks, put to death.

Surely with his acute intellect, Edgar must have been familiar with Thomas Jefferson's book, *Notes on the State of Virginia.* In it the Virginian wrote:

> There must doubtless be an unhappy influence on the manners of our people produced by the existence of slavery among us. The whole commerce between master and slave is a perpetual exercise of the most boisterous passions, the most unremitting despotism on the one part, and degrading submissions on the other. Our children see this and learn to imitate it . . . The parent storms, the child looks on, catches the lineaments of wrath, puts on the same airs in the circle of smaller slaves, gives a loose to his worst of passions, and thus nursed, educated, and daily exercised in tyranny, cannot but be stamped by it with odious peculiarities. The man must be a prodigy who can retain his manners and morals undepraved by such circumstances.

As much as Virginia was based on slavery, so was it based on racial prejudice. Masters always see their victims as inferior to themselves, and fit only for servitude. And then, quite conveniently, they turn this upside down and say, because these people are slaves, they are inferior.

It would not be long before that sense of superiority, the arrogance, and the concentration on one's selfish interests would begin to crop up in Poe's behavior, both within the family and beyond.

Like most boys, Edgar wanted to excel in sports. One classmate said he was "a swift runner, a wonderful leaper, and what was more rare, a boxer, with some slight training." But he showed off his athletic talent especially in swimming. When he was turning sixteen he won local fame by swimming 6 miles (over 9 kilometers) in the James River under a hot June sun, and for part of the way against a strong tide.

He liked to lead other boys in whatever he attempted, and found followers because of his reputation for skill and daring. He taught the son of Allan's partner how to shoot, swim, and skate, winning the boy's devotion.

As one of Poe's biographers, Kenneth Silverman, wrote, "In wanting to excel and to command, Edgar resembled many other orphans, in whom a feeling of nonexistence and the need to master changeable surroundings often produce a will for power." Even as he tried to stand independently and to lead others, he looked to Mrs. Allan for motherly warmth and support. But her nearly constant illness made it hard for her to fill that need, much as she wished to. He tried to find what he missed in Mrs. Jane Stanard, the mother of a schoolmate. When feeling blue and lonely, he went to her for consolation, coming to love her like an affectionate son. She too, however, was not well, often suffering from depression. Only a year after Edgar got close to her, she died of a brain tumor, at the age of thirty-one.

To young Edgar, Mrs. Stanard stood for an ideal of womanly grace. He was fond of calling her "Helen." When she died he was terribly upset, and was said to have visited her grave often. The memory of his mother's loss, and his mounting concern over Mrs. Allan's declining health, must have shaped his poems and stories linking beautiful women with illness, death, and loss.

Poe began writing poems dedicated to young Richmond girls. He also composed satires, one of which was a takeoff on the Junior Debating Society he belonged to. John Allan, who himself enjoyed poetry, liked to read with his foster son. He once remarked that "Edgar is wayward and impulsive . . . for he has genius . . . He will some day fill the world with his fame."

But Allan's warmth toward Edgar soon cooled. Grieving over the loss of Mrs. Stanard, Edgar displayed bleak moods and erratic behavior. As he neared sixteen, his defiance angered Allan. The boy seemed to him to have turned into a miserable mess—ungrateful and hostile. Yet hadn't Allan given him everything he needed or wanted, paying his tuition, buying good clothing, the best boots? But was it appreciated? "The boy possesses not a spark of affection for us, not a particle of gratitude for all my care and kindness towards him," Allan said. "I have given him a much superior education than ever I received myself."

3

The Teenager

AS EDGAR ENTERED HIS TEENS HE BEGAN studying in Richmond's schools. There was no free public education system at the time. Parents with the necessary funds sent sons to small private schools, each handling about twenty students. The courses offered included Greek and Latin, French, mathematics, science, and sometimes accounting and shorthand for those headed for the world of business.

Edgar's teachers were impressed by his gift for languages. He continued writing poems, reading some to his fellow students. One of them survives, a satire portraying a young lower-class clerk in a dry-goods store who dresses and behaves like one of the upper class. Edgar's envy of those above him and scorn for those he felt beneath him is all too clear.

He was proud of his verses, and when he had accumulated a fair number, he asked Mr. Allan to have them published as a book. But Edgar's schoolmaster advised against it, saying it would harm the youngster to be talked about so early as the author of a printed book.

When Poe did achieve prominence as an author, his classmates remembered him as competitive, eager for recognition, ambitious to excel, and quite bossy. One companion said that he hated anyone who tried to rival him.

John Allan had reason to feel troubled besides the challenge to his authority typical of adolescents like Edgar. For the past three years his business had known hard times, and huge debts had piled up, forcing the firm to declare bankruptcy.

By an unexpected twist of fate, everything changed abruptly. Allan's uncle, William Galt, was breakfasting in the Allan home one morning in 1825, when he sank back in his chair, and died. Galt, said to be the wealthiest man in Virginia, owned a large real-estate company, sawmills, stocks, plantations in several counties, and hundreds of slaves. He left everything to his nephew, John Allan. The estate amounted to nearly a million dollars, an enormous sum in those days.

Newly rich, and able to pay off his debts, Allan bought a mansion on the slope of a hill, centered among flower gardens,

THE ALLAN MANSION IN RICHMOND, VIRGINIA

grapevines, and fig trees, and with one of the best views in Richmond. The Allans lived in fine style, and entertained lavishly. With this turn for the better, it was natural for Edgar to think of himself as the heir to a great fortune and a prospect as pleasant and superior as the planters who lorded it over Virginia society.

In the loft of Mr. Allan's firm, which imported books, music, and periodicals, Edgar made himself familiar with trends in English and American literature and criticism. For a young man in a provincial city his cultural horizon was far broader than most others.

Always attentive to pretty women, Edgar began courting a neighborhood girl, Elmira Royster, a fifteen-year-old. With Edgar now enjoying wealth, he was at first welcomed into her home. The courtship advanced so rapidly that Elmira felt herself engaged to him.

Now sixteen and a half, it was time for Edgar to go on to college. The University of Virginia had opened only a year before. It was the fulfillment of Thomas Jefferson's old dream of establishing a great university, freely open to all. He believed that intelligence and ability were "sown as liberally among the poor as the rich." He got the state to acquire the land, himself drew the architectural plans, and took on the job of builder. But he failed to get the state to establish a complete system of education, from elementary school through college. Somehow, he said, the legislators didn't understand "that knowledge is power, and knowledge is safety, and knowledge is happiness."

Jefferson had once written that education should "be based on the illimitable freedom of the human mind. For here we are not afraid to follow truth wherever it may lead, nor to tolerate any error so long as reason is left free to combat it." Yet in appealing for support he played on intense sectional feelings aroused by the slavery issue, suggesting it was better that south-

AN ARTIST'S IMPRESSION OF TEENAGED ELMIRA ROYSTER

ern boys be educated in a southern university than at Harvard or Princeton, by "those who are against us in position and principle." He wanted the students to read only those specific authorities whose point of view he, Jefferson, endorsed. The faculty too must be "politically sound."

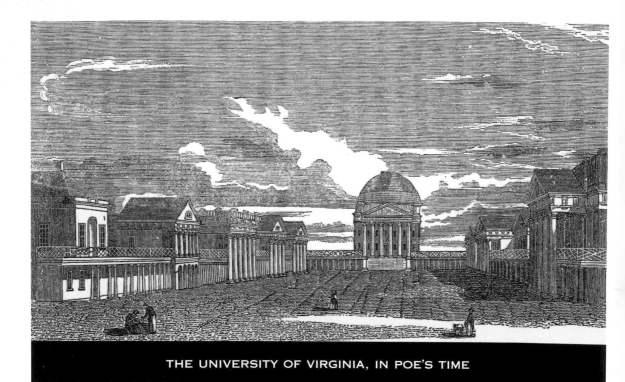

THE UNIVERSITY OF VIRGINIA, IN POE'S TIME

When the university opened in March 1825, Jefferson, at eighty-three, had not long to live. Yet Edgar, who arrived for his freshman year on Valentine's Day 1826, must have seen him when the great Virginian visited the campus. The university, still under construction, was located near the village of Charlottesville, 60 miles (96 kilometers) from Richmond. It was laid out like a village, along a broad quadrangle, with two-story buildings on each side. The professors lived on the upper floor, and classrooms were beneath. In the dormitories linking the pavilions lived the students, 177 the year Edgar entered. A rotunda-shaped library was being built at one end of the quadrangle.

Eight professors, chosen by Jefferson for their distinction, each headed one of the eight schools. Edgar enrolled in two of the schools—ancient languages and modern languages. He studied French, Italian, and Spanish. Allan had urged him to take math too, for practical business reasons, and when Edgar refused, was angry. The boy wanted to make a career in literature, not business or law or anything else. It seems Edgar didn't have to work hard to do well. Students noticed that he did little to prepare his lessons in advance. With only a few minutes of study, his superb mind and memory enabled him to stand up in class and outshine everyone else. He joined the Jefferson debating club, where he was applauded for his brilliant arguments. In athletics too he excelled, setting a mark of 20 feet (6 meters) in the broad jump. He continued to write poetry, which he read to his classmates.

What young Poe looked like at college one classmate has handed down to us: "He was of a rather delicate and slender mold, finely marked features, and eyes dark, liquid and expressive. He dressed well and neatly. He was a very attractive companion, genial in his nature." He was also described as never laughing heartily, and always with a melancholy face.

Poe's education did little to change his aristocratic views. According to Van Wyck Brooks, in his multivolume study of early American literature:

> Poe considered democracy a delusion and an evil. His writings were to bristle with allusions to the "rabble" and the "canaille," to democracy as "an admirable form of government—for dogs," to voting as "meddling" with public affairs and republican government as "rascally," while they also expressed contempt of the writer for "reform cranks" and "progress mongers." Poe had no faith, as he often said, in human perfectibility or the general notions of equality, progress and improvement.

Successful as he was in his studies, Edgar nevertheless sank into bleak moods at times. One likely cause was his disappointment with Elmira Royster. He wrote her ardently and often, but never got a reply. Later he would learn that her father strongly disapproved of his fifteen-year-old considering herself engaged to be married to a seventeen-year-old. He had been vigilant to intercept all Poe's letters, and to destroy them without her knowledge.

Edgar's friction with his foster father worsened while at college. Allan had given him money to cover board and tuition, but Poe spent it within days. Fancying himself in the role of a Virginia gentleman, he had run up over $2,000 in gambling debts, and in bills at the local shops. The campus life at this time was poorly disciplined. Jefferson was all for minimal rules and maximum self-government.

The students weren't up to his standard.

Many students were the sons of the plantation gentry. They dressed in the best, were waited on by slaves, went riding, gambled, held cockfights, rioted on drunken binges, tossed bricks and bottles at professors, broke windows. Edgar tried to do what they did, including their drinking. Some who would know him in later years thought his alcoholism started in his student days. One observer described how he tried to get drunk in the shortest possible time:

> Poe's passion for strong drink was as marked and peculiar as that for cards. It was not the taste for the beverage that influenced him; without a sip or smack of the mouth he would seize a full glass without water or sugar, and send it home with a single gulp. This frequently used him up.

Because Allan had not given him enough money to enjoy student life to the full, Edgar complained that he was regarded like a beggar. When he wrote him to ask for more money, Allan replied "with the utmost abuse," Edgar said, giving him so little he desperately tried to obtain funds by gambling, which only plunged him deeper into debt.

Allan did pay some of the debts he thought legitimate, but drew the line at Edgar's self-indulgence. When Edgar returned home for Christmas, Fanny Allan received him affectionately, but he was treated coldly by Allan. Elmira's parents told him that she was not in Richmond. She had in fact become engaged to a young man named Alexander Shelton, apparently believing Edgar had turned his back on her. The town had heard rumors of bad behavior at the university, and Edgar was shunned by some who had once been his warm friends.

You're not going back to college, Allan told him. I've had enough. In itself, just one year of college was no disgrace, for most students didn't stay any longer. The University of Virginia had not yet reached the point of granting degrees.

Why did Allan treat his foster son this way? He had willingly paid the boy's expensive schooling in London and in Richmond, at a time when his business was failing. But he sent him to college with all too little money, knowing it would surely cause trouble. Yet now he had come into a large fortune!

As he himself had come up the hard way, maybe Allan wanted to test the boy's ability to manage on his own, as he himself had once done. Or perhaps he didn't want Edgar to get used to an extravagant style of life. Then too, while he bragged of Edgar's talents, he might have been jealous of them. Another possibility is that Allen knew Edgar felt closer to Mrs. Allan than to him, and knew too that the boy resented the gossip caused by Allan's affairs with other women.

Whatever the reason, the break between the two seemed beyond repair. What was Edgar to do now with his life? Whether he chose to or was ordered to, he went to work clerking in Allan's firm, without pay. A job he hated, but to make things even worse, those he owed money to pursued him. He was even threatened with jail for nonpayment and still Allan, despite his wealth, would not help.

Two months after his return from the university, Edgar and his foster father had a slam-bang confrontation, and Edgar stormed out of the house. He found a room somewhere, and wrote Allan for money to pay his way north. Allan refused. Late in March 1827, now eighteen, Poe set out for Boston, his birthplace. He told Allan he had decided to find some place in the wide world where he would be treated decently, "not as you have treated me."

24

Soldier—and Poet

ALMOST PENNILESS, POE WORKED HIS PASSAGE north on a coal freighter. In Boston, he found work as a clerk in a waterfront warehouse and then on a small newspaper. Still trying to throw creditors off his trail, he created the myth that he had sailed off to Greece to join in its fight for independence from the Turks. That fantasy may have been sparked by current accounts of the young Boston physician, Samuel Gridley Howe, who was already in Greece aiding their War of Independence, and by the English poet Lord Byron who also had gone to Greece to serve the same cause and had died there of a fever. Still another fanciful rumor circulated that Poe had made his way to St. Petersburg, Russia.

Poe had carried the manuscript of some of his poems to Boston, and now showed them to a young printer whose family had probably known Poe's parents. That summer a forty-page booklet was published, titled *Tamerlane and Other Poems*. Written anonymously, and with only nine short poems and the long title poem, it drew almost no reviews. In a preface, Edgar claimed that the poems were composed when he was only thirteen.

VIEW OF BOSTON IN THE 1830s

Tamerlane is presented as the deathbed confession of the famous Mongol conqueror of the fourteenth century who saw himself as a genius pursuing his ambition. He had left his childhood sweetheart to conquer the world, but now has returned to his native village only to discover her dead, and his childhood dream vanished. That sense of loss, centered on the death of a beautiful woman, would recur in several of Poe's works to come. Edgar was casting himself in Tamerlane's role. His uncle James Galt had once said that Poe was "fully imbued in his early years with an idea that he would one day become a great writer."

Not to worry, Poe told the reader (and himself) if this volume is ignored. Failure wouldn't matter. He meant to be a poet, whatever the cost. In this self-analysis, Poe, like other young American poets of his day, was shaped by the image of Byron as the ambitious but lonely artist, now proud, now gloomy, with a temperament so out of tune with ordinary people.

When *Tamerlane* appeared, Poe was in the United States Army. Not under his own name, but as Edgar A. Perry (probably to evade creditors). It's likely he volunteered to serve because he had trouble making a living—a common enough reason then, and now too. But there was also a military tradition in his family. His paternal grandfather, David Poe, had won George Washington's praise for his work as a quartermaster in the Revolutionary Army. And Edgar himself, while at school in Richmond, had been a lieutenant in the Morgan Junior Riflemen. Now, finding himself lonely in Boston, the prospect of living as a soldier with other young men must have seemed a happy change.

We know little of Poe's life during the two years as a soldier. This was the quiet time between the War of 1812 and the war with Mexico of 1846. Military life was a dull routine of drill and housekeeping. Nevertheless, Poe accepted army discipline. His academic skills got him assigned to quartermaster duties and to company clerk. His pay was $10 a month. His officers praised him for prompt and faithful work. In contrast to his college year, he was "entirely free of drinking," an officer reported.

In his first six months, Poe served with an artillery unit at Fort Independence in Boston Harbor. Then his outfit was transferred to Fort Moultrie, South Carolina, 9 miles (14 kilometers) from Charleston. About six weeks later he was moved again, to Fort Monroe on the James River in Virginia.

On January 1, 1829, he was promoted to sergeant major for artillery. It was the highest rank a noncommissioned soldier could reach, just below second lieutenant.

Doing this well in the military, however, was not enough for the ambitious Edgar. He chose to quit. But how could he? Enlistment was for five years, and he had given only two. To his commanding officer, a fatherly man, he confessed his true name, that he had been orphaned early, and had troubles with his foster father. The sympathetic officer said he would permit the discharge, if Edgar reconciled with John Allan. In the end, Allan refused to help, advising that Edgar "had better remain as he is until the termination of his enlistment."

It seems Mr. Allan, upon becoming rich, had also become hardened. His own sisters felt he had abandoned them. When Edgar wrote him, again and again, he failed to answer. Edgar pleaded, "My father, do not throw me aside as degraded. I will be an honor to your name . . . Write me, my father, quickly." Again, no reply. Then Edgar tried another approach. He wrote again, this time asking Allan's help in entering the United States Military Academy at West Point.

Poe's letter showed that he was trying to make amends for the past. He no longer blamed Allan for messing up his college life by refusing him money. And he said how much he loved Fanny Allan, although he had not written her during those two years in the army. Unfortunately, it was too late. For Mrs. Allan, still suffering from a painful and lingering illness, was close to death. When he heard the news, Edgar rushed back to Richmond, but arrived on the night after her burial.

With his wife's death, Allan's harsh treatment of Edgar changed. He bought him a new set of clothes, and agreed to support his release from the army and entry into West Point.

On April 15, 1829, Edgar was discharged from the army, and a few days later, officers in his unit provided letters recommending him to West Point. But actual entry wasn't easy. There was a long waiting list for appointments to the academy, with forty-seven candidates ahead of Edgar.

While living in Baltimore, awaiting entry to West Point, Poe found that his grandmother was holding the family together. Living with her were her daughter Maria Clemm, Maria's seven-year-old child Virginia, and Poe's brother Henry. Edgar lodged in cheap rooming houses and spent some time with Henry. By this time his brother, wasting away with tuberculosis and drinking heavily, wasn't much of a companion.

Meanwhile, Poe continued to write. He created a second volume of poems that he induced a Baltimore publisher to print. His payment was to be 250 free copies. The book appeared in December 1829. Its title was *Al Aaraaf, Tamerlane, and Minor Poems.* It was seventy-one pages long, and this time, dropping his anonymity, he signed it Edgar A. Poe. Using only a middle initial he was acknowledging John Allan's name, yet refusing to give him full recognition.

"Al Aaraaf," with its 264 lines, is the book's longest poem, and hard to understand. Its title comes from the name of the star discovered in 1572 by the astronomer Tycho Brahe. Poe's melancholy suffuses the poem. It expresses "disillusionment with the world and escape into some more congenial realm of dream or of the imagination," as one critic said.

Among the shorter poems was "Sonnet—To Science," considered by some to be one of Poe's best. It laments how the "dull realities" of science have made obsolete the beautiful myths of true poetry. As in his "Tamerlane," the poet withdraws from the outside world to celebrate the subjective inner world. Poe would continue to insist that science and the imagination, reality and dream, truth and poetry, are in conflict.

Perhaps pleased that Edgar had published another volume of poetry, Allan made a gesture of reconciliation, asking Poe to come see him. In March 1830 the appointment to West Point came through. To obtain full release from the army however, Poe had to pay for a substitute. He had found a willing man, on the condition he pay him money for doing it. But when Edgar failed to send him the full sum, he was pressed for the rest of it. To explain the delay, Poe wrote that he was trying to get the money from his foster father, but that "Mr. A. is not very often sober." (Later, when Allan discovered what he'd said, he broke completely with Edgar.)

At this point in time, however, Allan bought Poe the outfit he needed, and gave him some money. Poe passed the entrance exams and on July 1 was enrolled at West Point with pay of $28 a month. He pledged to serve the United States for five years, unless released sooner.

5

In West Point, and Out

THAT SUMMER OF 1830, POE TOOK THE
routine drill at an encampment that West Point put all its new
cadets through before academic life would begin. The academy
at West Point, established in 1802, was built on highlands along
the west bank of the Hudson River, 50 miles (80 kilometers)
north of New York City. About 130 cadets were admitted each
year, but only about a fourth graduated. At twenty-two, Edgar
was older than the others, and with his experience at the university and in the army, he believed he'd do better than most.
The daily routine: You got up at 5 A.M., studied till breakfast at
7, and again from 8 to lunch, and again from 2 to 4 in the afternoon. That was followed by drill, parade, and supper. And
study again from 7 till bedtime at 9:30 P.M.

Edgar took French and advanced mathematics and gave
all day every day to mastering them. It was hard going, to con-
centrate for so many hours and days on just two courses. He
livened the routine by presenting himself to his classmates as a
young genius, the survivor of amazing adventures. So freely
and convincingly did his fancy roam that the cadets came to
believe he had truly led a life unmatched even in fairy tales. He

amused them in another way by writing verses satirizing their instructors.

While the academy demanded discipline, it also provided an extended family life. Your teachers were fatherly, and your fellow students brotherly. Life at the Point was more warm and intimate than anything the orphan had known before.

Edgar's ease of mind was shaken when disturbing news reached him. He knew that a woman Allan had had an affair with had recently borne him twins. And just when the widower was proposing marriage to a Miss Louisa Patterson. Allan's loose behavior was no secret in Richmond, and Miss Patterson said she'd accept him only if he reformed his ways. Apparently he assured her he would. Now Edgar learned that Allan had just married Louisa Patterson. At fifty-one, Allan was twenty years older than his second wife. After the childless years with his first wife, Allan could hope to father an heir to his fortune.

THE DRILL GROUND AT WEST POINT MILITARY ACADEMY

What it meant to Edgar was that others—the new wife and children sure to come—would enjoy the warmth and wealth he never had. He feared the door to Allan's home would be slammed shut. And by year's end, it was. Allan wrote Edgar what he called his final letter: He said he never wanted to hear from Edgar again.

Jolted by the letter, Edgar decided to quit West Point. This after only six months. He wrote home that he was too worn out, too sick—implying this was Allan's fault—to put up with the academy any longer. Since Allan had signed the application to West Point, committing Edgar to serve in the military for five years, he had to consent to Edgar's departure.

Allan refused. It seems he did not believe a word of Edgar's complaint of illness. And maybe now, newly married and expecting to have a son and heir of his own, he was glad to get rid of this troublesome "genius." Edgar insisted on going his own way. Under the academy's regulations, cadets could be dismissed on charges of bad conduct. Poe began neglecting his studies and his duties, piling up violations by the dozens.

On January 28, 1831, he was court-martialed on two major charges—gross neglect of duty and disobedience of orders. The military court found him guilty on all charges and ordered that "the cadet EA Poe be dismissed from the service of the United States."

Before he left West Point, Poe got many cadets to put up $1.25 each to cover the cost of printing a new edition of his poems. His classmates mistakenly believed the book would include satirical verses on their officers.

In February, Poe said his final good-bye to the military life and sailed down the Hudson to New York. There he contracted an acute ear infection. Sick and desperate, he appealed to Allan for help, and was ignored. In one of his outrageous romantic gestures, he wrote Colonel Thayer, the academy's commandant, who had liked the poet in spite of his behavior, and asked him for a letter recommending him for a military appointment to the commanders of the Poles fighting for their freedom from the Russians occupying their country. Nothing, of course, came of it.

In April a New York publisher issued *Poems by Edgar A. Poe,* dedicated "To the U.S. Corps of Cadets." The book includes the revised long works "Tamerlane" and "Al Aaraaf," plus six new poems. In a preface, Poe tells readers what he thinks a poem should be. His ideas derive from his reading of the English poet and critic Samuel Taylor Coleridge. Poe holds that a true poem is the opposite of both a work of science and a work of romance. As with "Sonnet— To Science" Poe challenges poets who try to teach or moralize in their work, and holds that the aim of the poet is the creation of pleasure.

Much verse of that time was romantic, and in Poe's poems there is gentle mockery of that spirit. One of his new poems (often to be reworked) was "To Helen." In it, the poet is a wanderer who longs to be home:

> On desperate seas long wont to roam,
> Thy hyacinth hair, thy classic face,
> Thy Naiad airs have brought me home
> To the beauty of fair Greece,
> And the grandeur of old Rome.

According to the biographer Kenneth Silverman, "Many lines in Edgar's three volumes . . . are cribbed or slightly reworked from poems by others." He therefore questions Poe's claim that he is always independent. Nevertheless, Silverman concedes that "his poems, taken as a whole and as a group, read as distinctly his."

Although the book drew a couple of favorable reviews, Poe found no work in New York and in May moved to Baltimore. Again, failure. He was turned down for a job on a local newspaper. Broke, as usual, he moved in with his aunt, Maria Clemm (his father's widowed sister), and her child, Virginia. They were all so pinched for money to meet living expenses that Poe helped his aunt to transfer her domestic slave to another master for a term of nine years. For this, they were paid $40. Most slaves in Baltimore at that time did domestic work, sometimes hired out to work for another.

To the family's heavy burden of poverty was added the pain of sickness and death. Edgar's brother Henry died on August 1, 1831. All around them people were dying, for a cholera epidemic was devastating communities along the East Coast.

Beyond that horror was the fear that a slave insurrection might erupt anywhere in the South. On August 22, 1831, Nat Turner, a Virginia slave and preacher, feeling he was called by God to lead "the children of Egypt" out of bondage, launched the greatest revolt the region would experience. With five others, he swore to massacre all the whites on nearby plantations. Their ranks swelled to some eighty others as they advanced. For almost two days they ravaged Southampton County, killing scores of white men, women, and children. The whole South was thrown into a panic. In retaliation, more than one hundred blacks, innocent or guilty, were struck down before the insurrection was crushed and Turner hanged. Throughout the region, amid widespread hysteria, many blacks were arrested and executed. That direct action by blacks, refusing to submit to their oppressors, fired the anti-slavery movement. On the other hand, it caused pro-slavery forces throughout the South to tighten controls on slaves and free blacks.

Poe, who had long identified himself with the aristocratic tradition of the slaveholders, probably felt justified in his pre-

THE CAPTURE OF NAT TURNER, LEADER OF A SLAVE UPRISING

tensions to racial superiority. It is ironic that he was living in Baltimore, not far from where fourteen-year-old Fred Bailey worked as a domestic slave. Six years later he would escape north and, under his adopted name, Frederick Douglass, begin his rise to international fame as a great writer, editor, and orator. Two talents, one white, one black. Each commanding extraordinary skill with words. But one standing for segregation and slavery; the other for freedom and equality.

In the summer of 1831 the Philadelphia *Saturday Courier* announced a $100-prize contest for fiction. Poe sent in five stories that were part of a sequence he planned. The prize went to another contestant, but the paper began to publish Poe's stories at regular intervals throughout 1832. They were all comic tales with many clever plays on words, and all dealt with ways of surviving death. The judges praised the young author for his "wild, vigorous and poetical imagination, a rich style, a fertile invention, and varied and curious learning."

All the stories satirized the popular fiction the magazines liked to run. It is uncertain whether he was paid for them; if he was, it must have been painfully little. For now, at twenty-three, he still had to rely on his family for a place to live. It was Maria Clemm who supported them by working as a dressmaker. Although Baltimore was a prosperous port city and shipbuilding center, Edgar failed to find work and would remain destitute for nearly three more years.

Poe continued to write short tales and verse and managed to get them printed. He helped the family by tutoring his young cousin, Virginia Clemm, becoming more and more attached to the child, who looked a lot like his mother. In April 1833, Edgar sent a letter to Allan, saying he was "absolutely perishing for want of aid" and begging to be saved from "destruction." Once more, no reply.

In June the Baltimore Saturday *Visiter* announced prizes to be given for best story and best poem. Poe sent in a poem and six stories from a group he called "The Tales of the Folio Club." There were two kinds of stories in his Folio Club collection: funny or terrifying. One of the comic pieces tells of a

MARIA CLEMM, AUNT AND MOTHER-IN-LAW OF POE

man who dies of shock when served food improperly and then plays cards with the Devil. In the other kind, Poe creates the scary scenes and action that would become his trademark.

A judge of the *Visiter* contest, John Latrobe, a Baltimore lawyer who met Poe at that time, left us this description of him:

> He was, if anything, below the middle size, and yet could not be described as a small man. His figure was remarkably good, and he carried himself erect and well, as one who had been trained to it. He was dressed in black, and his frock-coat was buttoned to the throat, where it met the black stock, then almost universally worn. Not a particle of white was visible. Coat, hat, boots, and gloves had very evidently seen their best days, but so far as mending and brushing go, everything had been done, apparently, to make them presentable. On most men his clothes would have looked shabby and seedy, but there was something about this man that prevented one from criticising his garments . . .

Getting his work into print did little to lift Poe out of poverty, although he was paid $50 for one of his stories.

Meanwhile, John Allan, who had ignored Edgar for the past three years, fell seriously ill, at age fifty-four. He now had two sons. In 1834, soon after the Allans had a third child, he died suddenly. He had not wasted the huge estate left him by his uncle, and Edgar anxiously awaited the disclosure of his will. One after the other came the names of those left parts of the estate, now estimated at about a million dollars.

To Edgar, his foster son, he left exactly nothing.

6

Satire and Science Fiction

HIS BAD LUCK COULD NOT GO ON FOREVER.
Or could it? Poe's pessimism had ample cause. Yet, at least for
a while, his luck was about to change.

America itself was changing in the 1830s. Still a nation
mostly of farms and small towns, it was beginning to see the rise
of large cities. An industrial revolution threatened to replace
small workshops with big factories such as the textile mills
springing up in New England. The typical American expected
to become a capitalist. For any hardworking, ambitious person,
enterprise was a kind of religion.

Andrew Jackson, in 1832, won a second term in the White
House on the wave of what one historian called "a frenzied race
for riches." His goal was to enlarge opportunities for individuals, without imposing government limits. Yet in the absence of
any controls, men, women, and children laboring in the new
factories worked from dawn to dark at pitiful wages and under
dreadful conditions. Liberal ministers preached to their con-
gregations that the rich were getting richer and the poor poorer.

To resist that trend, trade unions sprang up in most of the
nation's cities. They saw the need to unite for higher wages,

shorter hours, and better working conditions. And they were among the first to embrace social reforms. They wanted to abolish imprisonment for debt, for instance, a threat that Poe would face again and again.

As a tide of reform rose, it brought about many important changes in American life. A passion for education created the public school systems while it extended education to adults as well, a boon especially for immigrants flooding in from Europe. Advances in the technology of printing led to cheaper newspapers that would serve a much wider reading public. In 1833 it was possible for the New York *Sun* to drop its price to a penny a copy. In 1830 there were 36 daily papers. Twenty years later there were more than 250.

These changes opened wider the doors of opportunity for writers, who could submit their prose or poetry—or apply for an editorial job—to many publications. New York, Philadelphia, and Boston now became the nation's major literary centers. But the South too was in the running. In 1834 a Richmond printer, Thomas W. White, founded a new literary magazine, the *Southern Literary Messenger.* He helped to draw southern writers who would provide prose and poetry to entice southern readers. He wanted to divert southerners from a too intense focus on politics by exposing them to the pleasures of literature. While at the same time he wanted to attract northern subscribers.

THOMAS W. WHITE, PUBLISHER OF THE <u>SOUTHERN LITERARY MESSENGER</u>

In its first year, the *Messenger* earned praise from established literary figures, both North and South. Poe awoke to its possibilities for himself through a new friend, John Pendleton Kennedy. He was a Baltimore novelist known for his stories of plantation life, who had been a judge for the *Visiter* prize. He encouraged Poe to submit one of his stories, "The Assignation," to *Godey's Lady's Book*. The magazine published it anonymously in January 1834, marking Poe's debut in a journal of national standing.

Glad as Poe was to see his work in print, it did little to put money in his pocket. Kennedy tried and failed to get him a teacher's job in a Baltimore public school. Once when Kennedy asked him to dinner, Poe said he couldn't come because he looked too shabby. Kennedy thought he appeared to be starving, and lent him $20 to buy clothing so he could dine with him. Poe remarked that he felt so sick he could "hardly see the paper on which he wrote."

Securing a steady income, however modest, was necessary more than ever to Poe because he had fallen in love with his cousin Virginia, and wanted to marry her—although the girl was barely thirteen. They had become a tight-knit group, centered on Poe's Aunt Maria, a remarkable woman giving him the unfailing warmth and care he so desperately needed. At last he had a permanent family.

On Kennedy's urging, Poe began a correspondence with

JOHN P. KENNEDY, EARLY
SUPPORTER OF POE

White of the *Messenger,* offering him, tactfully, suggestions for what to run in the magazine. Don't think that readers like only simple, moralistic stuff, he said. The success of English magazines demonstrates readers really like "sensational subjects treated in a heightened style." Adding, "to be appreciated, you must be *read.*" He also offered White practical tips for designing and promoting the magazine.

Poe really had no personal experience to qualify him to give advice on a magazine enterprise. "But his air of expertise," said Silverman in his biography of Poe, "was well founded on a canny understanding of what interested the growing reading public. And much of his understanding in turn, came from his eager effort to find an audience for his own work."

White was impressed by Poe, and took him on as assistant editor in 1835 at a salary of $10 a week. Beyond that, whatever he wrote for the *Messenger* White paid for by the column. At last Poe had entered the literary world as a paid professional.

Glad as Poe was to take this step upward, it did not put much money in his pocket. Nor did it dispel the bouts of depression he so often suffered. It worried White too that Poe began drinking too much. He had left his family in Baltimore to take the editing job in Richmond. Lonely and distraught, when Maria Clemm wrote that Virginia might move into a cousin's home, he was frantic at the breakup of his family, and wrote back that he wanted to marry Virginia. Though twenty-six now, twice her age, there was no doubt that he loved his young cousin, but probably, at this time, only in a brotherly way.

In September, Poe quit his job at the *Messenger* and went back to Baltimore. First he took out a license to marry Virginia, giving her age as twenty-one (they weren't married until eight months later, in May 1836). Then he wrote White asking to be hired again. Only, replied White, if you promise never to get drunk. Poe agreed, and early in October brought Virginia and her mother to Richmond. They found rooms in a boarding house for $9 a week, leaving him but a single dollar in his pay.

For the family to survive, he had to add a lot to that dollar. He wrote, and wrote, and wrote. Within one year the *Messenger* published revised versions of his first seven stories, some new stories, more than a hundred book reviews and editorials, plus a column on doings in the literary world. And even more: a batch of satiric sketches about well-known authors.

An astonishing output, yet it was created while Poe carried on all his editorial duties: inviting writers to contribute to the *Messenger,* judging what they sent in, copyediting manuscripts, proofreading galleys, and following through on all the elements of printing and publication.

By December 1835, White was so pleased with Poe's work that he took a back seat, making Poe all but officially the real editor in chief.

Among Poe's new tales in the *Messenger* were three scary ones. In the first, "Berenice," the narrator is in love with Berenice, especially for her teeth, to the point of an obsession. When she "dies," he breaks into her tomb to retrieve her teeth, without realizing that she had been buried alive when in a cataleptic fit. Unaware that she is still living, he pries all thirty-two teeth out of her mouth. Critics have found the circumstances so absurd, they take it as Poe's poking fun at the kinds of stories popular in his time. Poe himself said he was only trying to show that he too could pull off the kind of story that helped sell magazines.

Another of his grotesque stories, "King Pest the First," is a political satire on President Andrew Jackson, the hero of the common man, and his pals in the "Kitchen Cabinet." Always fancying himself the aristocrat, Poe looked down upon the "rabble" so devoted to Jackson's brand of democracy.

VIRGINIA, POE'S YOUNG WIFE

Poe's first attempt at writing science fiction was "Hans Pfall," taking off from the intense public interest in the development of the hot-air balloon. (The first one to succeed flew above Paris in 1783.) Poe began his story with what seems to be a news report, but then shifts into clowning with elements of a fake science. He put two intense weeks of work into writing the story, mixing in details of actual fact to make the piece believable. Later he said it was a mistake to introduce comic elements, for it undermined the story's reality.

Modern science fiction would grow out of Poe's pioneering efforts. His vivid imagination took off from scientific facts to create plausible details, anticipating later discoveries in geography and astronomy. A host of science fictioneers like Jules Verne and H. G. Wells learned from Poe.

In his book reviews for the *Messenger,* Poe proved himself to be one of the best literary critics in the country. He helped to set high standards for American literature and didn't hesitate to attack inferior stuff. Of one novel, for example, he said "it should be read by all who have nothing better to do." Of another, it "is too purely imbecile to merit an extended critique."

A modern commentator, evaluating Poe's role in literary history, called his criticism "heroic." In his own time, however, Poe's blunt blows angered many who never forgave his harsh criticism. If his goal was to increase the circulation of the *Messenger,* he succeeded.

7
Editor, Novelist, Husband

DURING THE TIME POE WORKED FOR THE
Messenger, it had a difficult task dealing with the slavery issue.
The abolitionist movement had been galvanized by William
Lloyd Garrison's fiery insistence on immediate emancipation.
His paper, *The Liberator,* was banned or burned in the South.
White and Poe wanted to hold the support of their southern
readers, while not angering their northern readers. They chose
to walk a tightrope editorially by adopting a position called
"average racism." That is, choosing material "with a lukewarm
view of slavery," as the critic J. Gerald Kennedy put it, in the
hope of offending as few readers as possible.

Meanwhile, Poe tried to nourish the talents of his beloved
Virginia. He tutored her in languages and algebra, and
obtained the use of a piano and a harp to develop her love for
music. Visitors remarked that she had a voice of "wonderful
sweetness, and was an exquisite singer." She wrote poetry too.
In one set of verses, a Valentine for him (the initial letters spell
his name), she speaks of their isolated life and of her threaten-
ing sickness:

Ever with thee I wish to roam—
Dearest my life is thine.
Give me a cottage for my home
And a rich old cypress vine,
Removed from the world with its sin and care
And the tattling of many tongues.
Love alone shall guide when we are there—
Love shall heal my weakened lungs;
And Oh, the tranquil hours we'll spend
Never wishing that others may see!
Perfect ease we'll enjoy, without thinking to lend
Ourselves to the world and its glee—
Ever peaceful and blissful we'll be.

His seventeen months on the *Messenger* was one of the best times of Poe's life. He and Virginia were newlyweds, and although content in his domestic life and achieving national recognition as editor and critic, he began to drink again. He knew he was risking his job and endangering his family's welfare. Yet—for whatever complex reasons—he could not stop. Once he started, the slide downhill was rapid.

Drinking, in Poe's case, said those who knew him, could turn him into a madman—even after just one glass of wine. For Poe it was a fatal addiction, and he knew what it did to him. Once he said, "I have absolutely no pleasure in the stimulants in which I sometimes madly indulge. It has not been in the pursuit of pleasure that I have periled life and reputation and reason. It has been the desperate attempt to escape from torturing memories, from a sense of insupportable loneliness, and a dread of some strange impending doom." What it did to him he also sometimes put into his stories. One of his characters who drinks speaks of its negative effects, and regrets his own miserable behavior.

Poe's alcoholism began in his early years. He drank at the University of Virginia and again at West Point. He would drink while on the *Messenger* when his work piled too high and his income didn't meet the family's needs. Now we know from studies that alcoholism can be hereditary, that it runs in families. In Poe's family, both his father and brother drank too much, which must have contributed to their early deaths. Drinking in Poe's day was quite common, especially for men. They drank at home, in their clubs, at the taverns found everywhere.

Nevertheless, Poe must have done his job well, for the *Messenger*'s circulation climbed from 500 to 3,500, and White's annual profit amounted to $10,000. A lot of money for the owner, but not so much for the editor. Poe kept nagging White for more pay, and this, together with the drinking, led to Poe's getting fired in January 1837. In a friendly way, for White said the magazine was still open to his writing. Again and again, Poe would work hard to carry out an important responsibility and then sabotage it by his uncontrolled behavior.

While at the *Messenger*, Poe tried to get a publisher to issue his stories in book form. He was turned down by the Harper firm, the leading American publisher. Do a novel, a friend suggested, and they'll consider it. Poe took the advice and began to write what would be his one and only novel, *The Narrative of Arthur Gordon Pym.* The first two parts ran in the January and February 1837 issues of the *Messenger.*

In the hope of making it in America's largest publishing center, Poe moved his family to New York City. They found a tenement where Mrs. Clemm could take in boarders. But it was a bad time, for a major financial crisis erupted that year. Speculation had gone wild, corruption and mismanagement were widespread, banks collapsed, debt piled up mountainously, people lost jobs for long periods of time. The economic depression would drag on for six awful years.

Little is known about the Poes for the next year and a half. A friend reported they lived on bread and molasses for weeks at a time. Poe may have found temporary work as a printer. But his pen was not idle. He worked on *Pym,* hoping the big book would draw a big audience. Happily, Harper accepted it, and promised to publish it in the summer of 1838.

With *Pym,* Poe was deserting his natural talent for lyric verse, and for short stories that built rapidly to a strong climax. He believed that the writer should aim at a single, powerful emotional effect, obtainable only at a single sitting. With a novel's spun-out story, you could not do that. Yet Poe tackled *Pym* because he had no other choice. Harper had told Poe that his brief tales "would be understood and relished only by a very few—not by the multitude." And it was the multitude that the publisher was interested in.

Beginning around 1820, a mass market would come to dominate the publishing world. The same cutthroat competition that ruled the larger business economy took hold in the publishing of books, magazines, and newspapers. Authors had less and less control over what they wrote and its arrival in print. Poe spoke of being forced to labor in "the magazine prison house." Businessmen had taken over, and their judgment determined what would produce profit for their company. Literature was becoming "an article of commerce," like shoes or wheat.

"Writers in America between the close of the Revolution and the outbreak of the Civil War had a hard row to hoe," according to the literary historian Richard D. Altick. No early American author, apart from Washington Irving and James Fenimore Cooper, could live by his writings alone. The popu-

POE, IN HIS TWENTIES

lar British authors dominated the American scene, for there was no international copyright law to protect their work. American publishers pirated British authors at will. While American readers might benefit from low-priced access to authors like Charles Dickens, it made the writer's profession a very shaky one.

Disheartened by crass commercialism, Poe decided anyhow to satisfy the market's appetite by making a product a sales force could peddle. Confident in his own cleverness, he turned the novel into a hoax. *Pym* opens as a true account of adventure on the high seas by a young man just back from his voyage. It could sound plausible because the public was intensely interested in polar exploration. The press was carrying articles about plans for an American exploratory voyage to the Antarctic, subsidized by the government. To cash in on the excitement, Poe borrowed material from factual accounts of voyages to the South Seas, and worked in his invented extracts from diaries and logbooks. He used such details to make his story seem authentic, while his imagination provided the fantastic elements that his short tales so often displayed.

When the book, Poe's fourth, appeared in late July 1838, some reviewers took it seriously as a genuine travel book, expanding what the world knew of geography. Others grasped that it was a hoax, but praised the elements of fantasy one could expect from Poe. Poe himself in a private letter called it "a very silly book." Maybe potential readers agreed, for the sales of *Pym* were poor. Today, however, you can find it in several editions. A modern critic has called *Pym* "the archetypal American story of escape from family, domesticity, and feminine influence into those open, uncharted spaces where initiation and danger confirm the value of male companionship."

Pym, the novel's main character, edges closer and closer to the South Pole, on four sea journeys, two in small boats, two in larger ships. His adventures include being confined for days to a coffinlike box in the hold of a ship. He suffers an unending nightmare of demons, serpents, empty deserts. At one point he encounters a ghost ship manned by chattering corpses, and lands on an island where black natives massacre white explorers. Toward the book's closing, he drifts helplessly closer to the South Pole and as the water around him grows warm and milky there arises out of the vapor a huge human figure whose skin is "of the perfect whiteness of the snow."

Here the story cuts off. The editorial note explains that Pym (who is telling the tale) died suddenly, with the last chapters missing.

An editor of Poe's collected works has said that he sees the novel's real importance in the possibility that it inspired Herman Melville to some extent to write his novel *Moby Dick*. Critics today still debate the meaning of *Pym*. No doubt Poe would have been delighted with the literary controversy his "silly book" stimulated.

Poe decided in the spring of 1838 to move with his family to Philadelphia. The Quaker City had grown large enough to support nine daily newspapers and some weekly ones. A rich urban life included the University of Pennsylvania, the Academy of Fine Arts, theaters, a music hall, the State House, and a sprawling Navy Yard. One of the nation's first public high schools opened in Philadelphia that year. Especially attractive for Poe was the city's major role in book and periodical publishing.

In all that time in New York, Poe had earned not quite $150—or less than 16 cents a day. The sales of *Pym* were so poor it did nothing to improve the family's life.

Maybe now—in a new city—his luck would change . . .

8

Hoaxes and Horrors

THE POES RENTED A SMALL HOUSE ON THE west side of Philadelphia, but with a fair-sized garden. Poe took in Catterina, whom he described as "one of the most remarkable black cats in the world— . . . for it will be remembered that black cats are all of them witches." He bragged that she was smart and strong enough to open a latched door with a cunning leap on the latch.

In Philadelphia, Poe became friendly with a young doctor, Thomas D. English, who often visited the Poes. "I was impressed favorably with the appearance and manner of the author," Dr. English said. "He was clad in a plain and rather worn suit of black which was carefully brushed, and his linen was especially notable for its cleanliness. His eyes at that time were large, bright and piercing, his manner easy and refined, and his tone and conversation winning." Poe's wife, Virginia, just turned seventeen, he thought "a delicate gentlewoman, with an air of refinement and good breeding, and Mrs. Clemm had more of the mother than the mother-in-law about her."

Always strapped for cash, Poe looked beyond writing to earn some money. He tried for a while to learn the difficult craft of lithography. But it was so physically taxing it made him sick. Then he asked a writer friend, James K. Paulding, who had just been appointed Secretary of the Navy, to find him a job in his department: "any thing, by sea or land—to relieve me from the miserable life of literary drudgery to which I now, with a breaking heart, submit, and for which neither my temper nor my abilities have fitted me." But this too, as with all his efforts to find a job that didn't call for writing, came to nothing.

Poe arrived in Philadelphia just as the simmering conflict between the pro- and anti-slavery forces would explode. As the closest northern city to the slave South, Philadelphia had become a haven for fugitive slaves. By this time the city's black population had risen to 15,000, and anti-slavery activity had intensified. Abolitionists organizing aid to runaway slaves and boycotts of slave-produced goods infuriated the sizable pro-slavery groups, who burned down the abolitionists' new building, Pennsylvania Hall, just as the Poes arrived. Moving on the state legislature, the racists got through a new law disfranchising free blacks.

Poe, unlike writers such as Lowell, Whittier, or Whitman, had nothing to say against the mounting tide of racism. He zeroed in on the urgent need to feed himself and his family. When he did look beyond that horizon, he lashed out at the powerful business world. Popular taste, he liked to say, was being corrupted by the chase after profits. Himself a penniless poet, he assumed the airs of a Virginia aristocrat while scorning America's "aristocracy of dollars."

In 1837 a new periodical had appeared in Philadelphia called *Burton's Gentlemen's Magazine.* It was published and edited by William E. Burton, an actor and theater manager. It dished out the usual menu of fiction, poetry, and articles, stressing sporting news as well. Poe had noticed it when the editor gave *Pym* a negative review. Despite that, Poe asked Burton to

tains. This time too Poe stole long passages from authentic accounts of such adventures. He apparently had no scruples about accusing other authors of such plagiarism. He was so skillful at these hoaxes that "The Journal of Julius Rodman" was cited as a factual reference in a Senate document of 1840 on the Oregon Territory.

In September 1839, *Burton's* published what some consider Poe's masterpiece, "The Fall of the House of Usher." It is one of his most famous works, a classic tale of horror. He tells the story of a twin brother and sister, Roderick and Madeline, the last descendants of a cursed family coming to its end in their haunted mansion.

From the first sentence, Poe creates a dark and menacing mood. He carries it out with a terrified narrator, underground passages, opium dreams, tubercular heroine, collapsing buildings, burial alive and the return from the grave—using many of the typical tricks of what are called "Gothic" tales. But Poe rises above them by making readers believe they are inside a tempestuous and doomed mind.

Within the tale is Usher's poem about his fear of going mad, "The Haunted Palace," which plays on the resemblance between Usher's face and the face (façade) of the house. In both story and poem, Poe portrays how frail the rational mind is, how subject to moral and psychological decay.

With the appearance of "The Fall of the House of Usher," Poe solidified a reputation as a writer to be taken seriously. It led to a Philadelphia firm agreeing to publish a two-volume edition of 25 of his stories, called *Tales of the Grotesque and Arabesque.* (By "grotesque" Poe meant comic or satiric, and by "arabesque," serious and poetic.) The publisher offered Poe no royalties, only the copyright and 20 free copies. With the depression still harrowing the country, they issued an edition of 750, taking three years to sell it out.

Reviews of the book were contradictory. One critic said the book was made up of "a wild, unmeaning, pointless, aimless set of stories, outraging all manner of probability . . . nonsense run mad." But another reviewer called the stories "a playful effusion of a remarkable and powerful intellect." Best of all for Poe was the *New York Mirror's* praise of his "power for vivid description, an opulence of imagination, a fecundity of invention, and a command over the elegances of diction which have seldom been displayed, even by writers who have acquired the greatest distinction in the republic of letters." In another favorable review, a Philadelphia critic noted how original Poe's work was, and said it compared favorably with the work of Coleridge, the highly esteemed English author.

Like all writers, Poe delighted in praise. One of his friends said that "no man living loved the praises of others better than he did." And like many other writers, he would use his natural skill in public relations to promote his work and himself. Writing anonymously he would promote in one magazine a story of his appearing in another magazine.

In another tale for *Burton's,* Poe drew for useful details on his childhood experience in England's schools. "William Wilson" is a thriller, a psychological study of a person who comes across someone else born on the same day, and sharing his height and appearance. As often happens with many authors, Poe gives Wilson some of his own physical and mental characteristics.

One of France's foremost poets and critics, Charles Baudelaire, praised Poe highly for "The Hidden Palace." Poe, he wrote, has clearly seen in man "a natural wickedness . . . a nameless force" without which "a host of human actions will remain unexplained, inexplicable," He called it a "natural perversity" that makes people do all sorts of terrible things.

Working for *Burton's* didn't meet the family's needs, so Poe began writing a column for the Philadelphia paper, *Alexander's*

Weekly Messenger. He published articles on ciphers, puzzles, and codes, challenging readers to stump him with cryptograms. He himself was only a novice at this, but readers of the family paper didn't know better. Whether his contributions were responsible or not, the circulation of both *Alexander's* and *Burton's* increased.

In June 1840, after just one year at *Burton's*, Poe left the magazine. He had little respect for it, and even less for its publisher. He thought much of what Burton ran was poor stuff, and disliked having his name associated with it. Nor did he like the fact that Burton had advertised his magazine for sale, without informing Poe, who had dreams of getting control of his own publication. There was an exchange of nasty letters between the two, and when Poe quit, he announced he would launch his own monthly journal, *The Penn Magazine.* No politics or moralizing, he promised, just literature.

He wanted it to be of high quality and sought for subscriptions at $5 a year. At that price and in hard times money was hard to come by. He would cling to his dream of owning his own magazine, but it would never be fulfilled.

Early in 1841 Poe was forced—or lucky!—to find work as literary editor of a new publication, *Graham's Magazine.*

The First-Ever Detective Story

IN THE LONG MONTHS BETWEEN LEAVING
Burton's and joining *Graham's*, Poe spent a lot of time hunting for subscribers to his own magazine. But failing to find enough, he took to liquor again. He drank so much that his friend Thomas English found him lying stupefied in the gutter and had to carry him home. Yet in the same period, he started writing a kind of story that had never before been tried in the history of fiction.

The owner of *Graham's,* a lawyer younger than Poe, offered him $800 a year—$300 more than his salary at *Burton's*—and a small page rate for his own writing. He sweetened that by relieving him of the routine chores an assistant editor would take care of. The magazine carried short stories, poems, essays, book reviews. It reached out to women by running fashion illustrations in color. With surprising speed, Poe's fine editorial hand boosted circulation from 5,000 to 40,000 within a year. The magazine became the most popular in America. It made Graham rich, but he would give up none of it to raise Poe's pay.

Poe kept contributing provocative reviews and articles and bringing in other good writers. He enticed subscribers by devices that made them active participants in the magazine. He ran a series showing how to read personality by studying signatures. He got readers to send in ciphers—a method of secret writing that substitutes other letters or characters for the letters intended, or transposes the letters after arranging them in blocks or squares. He challenged people to devise ciphers using any of several languages, and demonstrated he could solve them all. He believed "human ingenuity cannot conceive a cipher which human ingenuity cannot resolve." Of course he chose the ones to solve and publish.

In April 1841, *Graham's* published Poe's "The Murders in the Rue Morgue." It was the first detective story ever to see print, and it changed the course of world literature. It was the archetype for the modern detective story. Sir Arthur Conan Doyle, who in 1887 created Sherlock Holmes, the most famous detective in fiction, said that Poe "was the father of the detective tale, and covered its limits so completely that I fail to see how his followers can find any fresh ground which they can confidently call their own."

GEORGE R. GRAHAM, WHOSE MAGAZINE POE MADE A GREAT SUCCESS

At the heart of "Rue Morgue" is the detective Auguste Dupin, perhaps Poe's most interesting character. He is a Frenchman with an analytical mind who loves to tackle problems with his superior intellect. He combines scientific logic with the artist's leap of the imagination. Dupin (like Poe) is raised in a rich family but has fallen on hard times. Dupin has a companion—like Sherlock Holmes's Watson—who is slow-witted and needs to have everything explained. This of course shows us how brilliant Dupin is. He observes facts, analyzes them, and deduces their meaning. It was a recognizable, repeatable method that gave the detective the central role in the solution of crime whether in real life or in the detective fiction to come.

The clues that puzzle the police Dupin sees in a new way, and he discloses the solution to the mystery. The story had many of the elements that would come to delight fans of detective stories: the brilliant amateur detective, the clumsy cops, the naive pal. Poe's story and the several others like it he would write are examples of ratiocination, meaning the process of exact thinking.

In the same month "Rue Morgue" was published, Poe met a man who would influence public opinion of Poe long after the writer's death. He was Rufus Griswold, a Vermonter six years young than Poe. He was just building a name for himself by compiling popular literary anthologies. A bitter man with a harsh tongue, he could be vindictive with anyone who crossed him. When his *The Poets and Poetry of America* appeared in 1842, it included only three poems by Poe, but far more poems by writers now long forgotten. The two men wanted something from one another: Poe to be included in the anthologies, Griswold to obtain Poe's literary praise. Each would be hypocritical with the other. Griswold smeared Poe behind his back, and Poe, while seeking the man's favor, called him an outrageous humbug to others. Later, Poe savaged Griswold's character and

5

and from certain urgencies connected with this explanation I was aware that you could not have forgotten it. It was clear, therefore, that you would not fail to combine the two ideas of Orion & Chantilly. That you did combine them I saw by the character of the smile which passed over your lips. You thought of the poor cobler's immolation. So far, you had been stooping in your gait — but now I saw you draw yourself up to your full height. I was then sure that you reflected upon the diminutive figure of Chantilly. At this point I interrupted your meditations to remark that as in fact he *was* a very little fellow — that Chantilly — he would do better at the Théâtre des Variétés."

Not long after this we were looking over an evening edition of "Le Tribunal" when the following paragraphs arrested our attention.

"Extraordinary Murders. This morning, about three o'clock, the inhabitants of the Quartier St Roch were aroused from sleep by a succession of terrific shrieks, issuing apparently from the fourth story of a house in the Rue Morgue, known to be in the sole occupancy of one Madame L'Espanaye and her daughter Mademoiselle Camille L'Espanaye. After some delay occasioned by a fruitless attempt to procure admission in the usual manner, the gateway was broken in with a crow-bar, and eight or ten of the neighbours entered, accompanied by two gendarmes. By this time the cries had ceased; but as the party rushed up the first flight of stairs, two or more rough voices in angry contention were distinguished, and seemed to proceed from the upper part of the house. As the second landing was reached, these sounds, also, had ceased, and every thing remained perfectly quiet. The party spread themselves, and hurried from room to room. Upon arriving at a large back chamber in the fourth story (the door of which, being found locked with the key inside, was forced open) a spectacle presented itself which struck every one present not less with horror than with astonishment.

The apartment was in the wildest disorder — the furniture broken and thrown about in all directions. There was only one bedstead; and from this the bed had been removed, and thrown into the middle of the floor. On a chair lay a razor besmeared with blood. On the hearth were two or three long and thick tresses of grey human hair, also dabbled in blood, and seeming to have been pulled up by the roots. Upon the floor were found four Napoleons, an earring of topaz, three large silver spoons, and three smaller of metal d'Alger, and two bags containing nearly four thousand francs in gold. The drawers of a bureau, which stood in one corner were open, and had been, apparently rifled, although many articles still remained in them. A small iron safe was discovered under the *bed* (not under the bedstead). It was open, with the key still in the door. It had no contents beyond a few old letters, and other papers of little consequence.

Of Madame L'Espanaye no traces were here seen; but, an unusual quantity of soot being observed in the fire-place, a search was made in the chimney, and (horrible to relate!) the corpse of the daughter, head downward, was dragged therefrom, it having been thus forced up the narrow aperture for a considerable distance. The body was quite warm. Upon examining it many excoriations were perceived, no doubt occasioned by the violence with which it had been thrust up and disengaged. Upon the face were many severe scratches, and upon the throat dark bruises, and deep indentations of finger nails, as if the deceased had been throttled to death.

After a thorough investigation of every portion of the house without farther discovery, the party made its way into a small paved yard in the rear of the building, where lay the corpse of the old lady with her throat so entirely cut that, upon an attempt to raise her the head fell off and rolled to some distance. The body, as well as the head, was fearfully mutilated — the former so much so as to scarcely to retain any semblance of humanity.

To this horrible mystery there is not as yet, we believe, the slightest clew."

The next day's paper had these additional particulars.

"The Tragedy in the Rue Morgue. Many individuals have been examined in relation to this most extraordinary and frightful affair."

A PAGE OF POE'S MANUSCRIPT FOR "THE MURDERS IN THE RUE MORGUE,"
CONSIDERED TO BE THE FIRST DETECTIVE STORY

**RUFUS GRISWOLD, EDITOR OF A POETRY
ANTHOLOGY THAT INCLUDED POE**

intellect in a review of one of his anthologies. Their mutual hostility would have a strange outcome in years to come.

In 1842 the Poes were living in a small row house near Philadelphia's Fairmount Park. While Maria and Virginia did their best to keep the rooms clean and orderly, the family's poverty was plain to any visitor. They celebrated Poe's thirty-third birthday on January 19. The next evening, disaster struck. Virginia was singing and playing the piano when a blood vessel burst in her lungs and she almost drowned in the blood pouring from her mouth. Miraculously, she recovered, but only partially. The ruinous effect of her TB persisted; she would suffer continually in the five years left to her.

Virginia needed the greatest care as an invalid, care almost impossible to provide in such cramped, close quarters and with little money to find better living conditions or meet Virginia's mounting medical expenses. Her long-drawn-out illness, a visitor noted, had a devastating effect on Poe, "who was so sensitive and irritable . . . he would not allow a word about the danger of her dying—the mention of it drove him wild." Increasingly, Poe would act wildly, go on drinking binges, and express murderous rage in his tales.

Yet somehow he managed to continue writing. Several of his best stories appeared in the early 1840s. Auguste Dupin figures again in "The Mystery of Marie Rogêt," which was based on an actual murder that occurred in 1841 in Manhattan. "The Gold Bug," using Poe's knowledge of cryptography, won a $100 prize from a newspaper, and down the years has proved to be his most popular story.

In "The Pit and the Pendulum," the captive narrator is in a dark dungeon, nearly driven mad by thirst and hunger, and the fear of a razor-sharp pendulum that threatens to slice him to death.

"The Masque of the Red Death" deals with aristocrats fleeing to avoid a plague. Here Poe drew upon the cholera epidemic he had observed in Baltimore in 1831 and on his wife's terrifying hemorrhage to describe the symptoms and the swift ending of the victims:

There were sharp pains, and sudden dizziness, and then profuse bleeding at the pores, with dissolution. The scarlet stains upon the body and especially upon the face of the victim, were the pest ban which shut him out from the aid and from the sympathy of his fellow-men. And the whole seizure, progress and termination of the disease, were the incidents of half an hour.

In "The Black Cat," Poe once again portrays murderers, mad-men—and alcoholics. The narrator has a black cat as wise as the witches and popularly believed to be the Devil in disguise. Like Poe, the narrator is aware of his perverse nature. He too has seen the wealth he once enjoyed disappear, forcing him to live in poverty—and with a wife who is "the most patient of sufferers."

There is no doubt that Poe's was a superior intellect. He knew it and was proud of it. Yet he was both ashamed and furious that necessity bent him to the will of editors and publishers whose abilities he had only contempt for. "To write well," he said, "the man of genius must write in obedience to his impulses." When forced to disobey them, and to write at all hours and on anything and everything, it is no wonder he may create junk.

In his frequent book reviews for *Graham's,* Poe took on the great as well as the lesser writers. Novels by Charles Dickens were published (pirated!) in America in serial form as they were in England. In May 1841, Poe reviewed Dickens's *Barnaby Rudge.* When only the first chapters had been published, Poe predicted the identity of the murderer, still concealed by Dickens. He had the nerve to claim he knew better than Dickens, England's most famous writer, how his story would turn out.

Later, in reviewing the complete novel, Poe praised Dickens but pointed out what he saw as flaws in the story. Don't call a book great just because the writer is famous, he told his readers. Fame can't be the criterion for quality. This was a common aspect of Poe's reviews. He liked to play "one up" on other writers, be they Dickens, Hawthorne, Longfellow, or whomever. He held back on total praise, as if to say none of them is better than I am.

Poe would meet Dickens in May 1842, when the novelist, then thirty, was on his first American lecture tour. Dickens granted him two interviews at a Philadelphia hotel. They talked about American poetry and Poe asked him for help in getting a revised edition of his *Tales* published in England. This Dickens promised to do. He kept his word upon returning home, and talked about Poe to several publishers, but all refused to take on Poe. Nevertheless, the two remained friendly, and later, after Poe's death, when Dickens revisited America, he sought out Poe's Aunt Maria Clemm and offered her help.

In April 1842, Poe resigned from *Graham's* and Rufus Griswold took his job. Poe said he quit because he was disgusted "with the namby-pamby character of the magazine—the contemptible pictures, fashion-plates, music and love tales. The salary, moreover, did not pay me for the labor I was forced to bestow." Perhaps too he could not forgive Graham, who, on the day after Virginia's hemorrhage, had curtly refused to give him an advance on his pay to help him meet the crisis.

Upon leaving *Graham's,* Poe again slid rapidly downhill. He had stopped heavy drinking for some time, but his fear of losing Virginia at any moment, and the intense pressure of constant writing to meet their expenses, sent him off on binges. One friend said it was agonizing to see him "going headlong to destruction, moral, physical, and intellectual."

10

A Popular Lecturer

AGAIN, AS OFTEN HAPPENED WITH POE, HE managed to pull himself together and to try once more to launch his own magazine, now to be called *Stylus*. He asked prestigious writers if they would contribute work—men such as Cooper, Irving, and even Longfellow (whom he had publicly accused of plagiarism). Upon a friend's suggestion he put out feelers to President John Tyler for a government appointment, any kind, even for as little as $500 a year, something to keep him going.

In March 1843 he went to Washington, hoping to see the president, who, he was told, was "remarkably fond of poetry and music." Several authors would be given government posts—Hawthorne and Melville among them. If not too demanding, a job at the Philadelphia Custom House would not only provide steady income but time to do his own writing. It was hinted that if he got a post, his new magazine would be expected to publish pieces supporting the president's policies.

Away from the care of Virginia and her mother, Poe turned his week in Washington into a disaster. He drank too much and too often, had to borrow money for meals, dressed wildly, offended and even insulted friends who could have helped in his job hunt, and never got an appointment with the president.

Early in 1843, Poe's work began to appear in a new Boston magazine, *Pioneer.* It was started by a young Harvard graduate, James Russell Lowell, whose poems Poe had published in *Graham's,* predicting Lowell would become one of America's best poets. Like Poe, Lowell wanted to avoid the trashy stuff that peppered the pages of the popular magazines. When Poe offered to write for him, Lowell promised to pay $10 for each piece. The first three issues carried Poe's story "The Tell-Tale Heart," his poem "Leonore," and an article on writing verse.

"The Tell-Tale Heart" is a chilling murder story. It is told from the killer's point of view, and illustrates the desire to exercise power over an adversary. It is not a whodunit. The reader knows from the start who the murderer is. The psychology of the killer is what Poe focuses on.

Bad luck hit both Lowell and Poe. The magazine, up against a host of new ones, failed after its third issue, leaving Lowell deep in debt and Poe with the loss of a promising outlet. But broke as he was, Poe generously wrote Lowell not to worry about paying him the $30 he was owed.

It was mostly the Philadelphia publications that carried Poe's work, and far more often his tales than his poems.

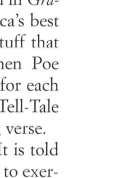

JAMES RUSSELL LOWELL, WHOSE BOSTON MAGAZINE PUBLISHED POE'S WORK

In June 1843 his "The Gold Bug" won a $100 prize from a local paper, and shortly after a dramatization of it was presented at a local theater. The prize money was a godsend, though not nearly enough to sustain the family.

In desperation, Poe decided to look into a new source of income—speaking to public audiences. This, though he had earlier put down what he termed "the present absurd rage for lecturing." The lyceum system, as it was called, arose out of the habit of American parents in the early 1800s to read aloud to the family from the works of authors. By the early 1830s this admirable custom had bloomed into the lyceum system. People wanted to be instructed or entertained by standing or sitting among many fellow listeners, concentrating on what some notable person had to say. This reliance on the spoken word arose long before people had easy access to newspapers, magazines, radio, television, movies. It soon became a source of income important to writers, thinkers, crusaders for social change—to anyone seeking self-improvement.

A lyceum would organize paid-in-advance lectures at regular intervals. Each time a different speaker would appear to talk on a different topic. By the mid-1830s there were about three thousand such lyceums, mostly in the North. The point was not only educational but social. In towns without the cultural or entertainment attractions we enjoy today, just getting together once a week—meeting old friends and making new ones—was a pleasure to look forward to.

As the lyceum movement spread, it drew many eminent men from across the ocean. British writers like Dickens and Thackeray reached American audiences on national tours. Here at home, Emerson, Thoreau, and Holmes were only a few among many prominent writers who found the lyceum economically important to them.

POE AT ABOUT **35**, SPORTING HIS NEW MUSTACHE

Poe of course was well aware of how profitable this might be for him, and he began writing to lyceum committees in the hope of setting up a series of lectures for himself. It worked: Within the next few months he would speak in Philadelphia, Newark, Wilmington, Baltimore, Reading. Popular interest in this odd author was so intense that hundreds couldn't get seats at the first lecture in Philadelphia.

Although he had sneered at lyceums, he worked hard to make a good showing, gathering good reviews everywhere. He was praised for his eloquence, graceful manner, and good voice. The title he used for his lectures was "The Poetry of America." But he went beyond the poetry sometimes to attack the poet. And especially Rufus Griswold, whom he treated with bare knuckles.

Even though he would speak for two hours, audiences didn't mind. (They were used to it. Later, political candidates like Abraham Lincoln and Stephen A. Douglas would debate the issue of slavery before audiences of 15,000 people standing outdoors for many long hours, reveling in the oratory.) Poe gossiped about infighting in the literary world, discussed the function of criticism, and recited some of his poems. Good show, the audience felt.

Now thirty-five, Poe got rid of his side-whiskers and grew the dashing mustache most remember him with. Conscious of personal appearance, he made fun of that concern with a sketch he published called "The Spectacles." It's about a man who is too vain to wear his eyeglasses, and with faulty vision is overwhelmed by the beauty of a woman—who turns out to be not only elderly but his own grandmother.

It seemed time to see if he could do better outside Philadelphia. He made a deal with a local paper called the *Columbia Spy* to write a series of pieces about life in the big city—New York. In April 1844, once again, the Poe family moved to New York.

11

New York: The Rich and the Poor

NEW YORK WAS A BRUTAL, RUTHLESS, tumultuous town in the 1840s. A necklace of piers, wharves, docks, and ships circled Manhattan below 14th Street. Some three thousand ships sailed or steamed into the harbor from at least 150 foreign ports. Barrels, sacks, boxes, bales, hogsheads piled high in the streets. Sailors seemed to threaten invasion. Hacks, carts, wagons, omnibuses, cabs competed for space on the cobblestoned streets as they toted supplies or passengers. The noise was shattering as iron horseshoes struck the pavements and drivers shouted and cursed for room to get by. The streets were lined by a jumble of wood, brick, and stone buildings.

And the noise, the noise! Steam ferries whistling, chimney sweeps crying their services, newsboys hawking the penny papers, bells on the ragpickers carts . . .Wide Broadway ran from the Battery south to 4 miles (6 kilometers) north, edged by gutters where black pigs rooted and snorted and stank.

By the time Edgar Allan Poe arrived in 1844, this busiest and wealthiest of all American cities claimed some 350,000 inhabitants. The contrast between rich and poor was blatant. The rich had migrated from the tip of Manhattan to build their mansions near City Hall, and some even further uptown to the foot of Fifth Avenue and Washington Square. The Massachusetts reformer Lydia Maria Child, editing an anti-slavery paper in the city, was also writing a column on New York life for a Boston paper. She reported on the human wrecks she saw everywhere in New York's streets. In the Five Points slum district she saw every form of human misery, every sign of human degradation—thievery, prostitution, murder. Dog-killers hired by the city roved the streets, slaughtering three hundred stray animals in just one day.

Manhattan's great hotels—the Astor, the Metropolitan, the St. Nicholas—were filled with southern planters and merchants. It was still a short time since slavery had finally ended in New York, in 1828. But there were New Yorkers even then

A BUSY STRETCH OF BROADWAY, NEW YORK

who owned slaves in the South, and a number who secretly thrived on the illicit slave trade.

Poe arrived in the city dead broke but optimistic. At age thirty-five he believed he could rebuild a career as a magazine editor and writer. His first task was to find a place for the family to live. They took rooms in a cheap boardinghouse at 130 Greenwich Street, in lower New York, near the Hudson River. It was then in the heart of the city. Although the old house was "buggy-looking," the landlady and her husband were nice and the food was great—"no fear of starving here!" He had only $4.50 and had to make or borrow enough somewhere, somehow, to get by.

But Poe's hope of living in the city petered out in only two months. He found the streets "insufferably dirty" and the noise "intolerably a nuisance." Seeking better surroundings, they moved to the 200-acre (80-hectare) Brennan farm 5 miles (8 kilometers) outside of town, near what is now 84th Street and Broadway. Poe enjoyed rambling around the woods and streams of the farm. But this country life won't last long, he predicted; it is doomed. The lovely Hudson waterfront hereabouts will be lined with "nothing more romantic than shipping, warehouses and wharves."

Though he disdained the city, he had to look to it for his livelihood. It meant doing hackwork—commercial journalism—not poetry or fiction. For that small-town Pennsylvania paper, the *Columbia Spy,* he wrote a series of pieces about big-city life called "Doings of Gotham." He even knocked out a campaign song for the 1844 election, producing five stanzas and a chorus in fifteen minutes, to the amazement of the politician who paid for it.

For the *Democratic Review,* a young magazine aimed at the rising generation of young Democrats, he wrote a series of short pieces called "Marginalia." Although he was scrabbling for a living, he portrayed himself as the comfortable book lover, generously furnishing readers with choice tidbits from his cultural table. His comments reflect his wide reading and his acute powers of observation.

Another outlet for Poe's work was the *New York Mirror,* one of whose editors was Nathaniel Parker Willis, the most successful magazine writer the country had yet seen. (Though few would know his name today.) Willis was paid $100 for each of his articles, earning around $5,000 a year—a millionaire's income in Poe's eyes. Willis made no pretense to being a literary artist, admitting that "I am obliged to turn to account every trumpery thought I can lay my wits to. My rubbish, such as it is, brings me a very high price."

Driven to extremes, Poe was forced to save his family from

NATHANIEL PARKER WILLIS, AN EDITOR OF THE <u>NEW YORK MIRROR</u>

hunger or eviction by grinding out trash as well as master-pieces. Whichever it was, he got paid the same for it at the usual space rates. In the three years after he quit *Graham's,* his work earned him only $121. His biographer Jeffrey Meyers estimates that his total income from all his books, over a period of some twenty years, amounted to less than $300.

Again and again he pressed friends and even strangers for help. Lend me five, lend me thirty, no, I'll take just twenty . . . His appeals became so constant, so demanding, that people hated to open his notes and often would refuse him. Commenting on writers' income, Poe once said that even garbagemen make more. He lashed out at the profit-hungry powers that ran the world:

> When shall the artist assume his proper situation in society—in a society of thinking beings? How long shall he be enslaved? How long shall mind succumb to the grossest materiality? How long shall the veriest vermin of the Earth, who crawl around the altar of Mammon, be more esteemed of men than they, the gifted ministers to those exalted emotions which link us with the mysteries of Heaven?

Poe began working at *The Evening Mirror* in the fall of 1844. Its offices were in the city's downtown. He had to walk the 5 miles from the Brennan farm to get to work each day. His pay was $15 a week. He liked Willis; though he knew his writing was trifling stuff, he respected the man's decency. Poe did his miscellaneous small chores reliably, and always on time, never resenting the trivia he was asked to pour out.

This was a paper catering to the world of society, the "frivolous and the fashionable." He wrote no piece for the *Mirror* under his own name. One of his unsigned articles, however, did deal with an important issue—the need for an international copyright law. The year before Poe came to the city, several writers had launched the American Copyright Club, headed by the poet and editor William Cullen Bryant. The club attacked literary piracy as a crime and called for passage of laws against it. Most publishers opposed such a measure. They argued that because they were free to publish anything they chose, it made a great deal of literature cheaply available to American readers. The club soon died. No international copyright law would be adopted until 1891. "Without an international copyright law," Poe said, "American authors may as well cut their throats."

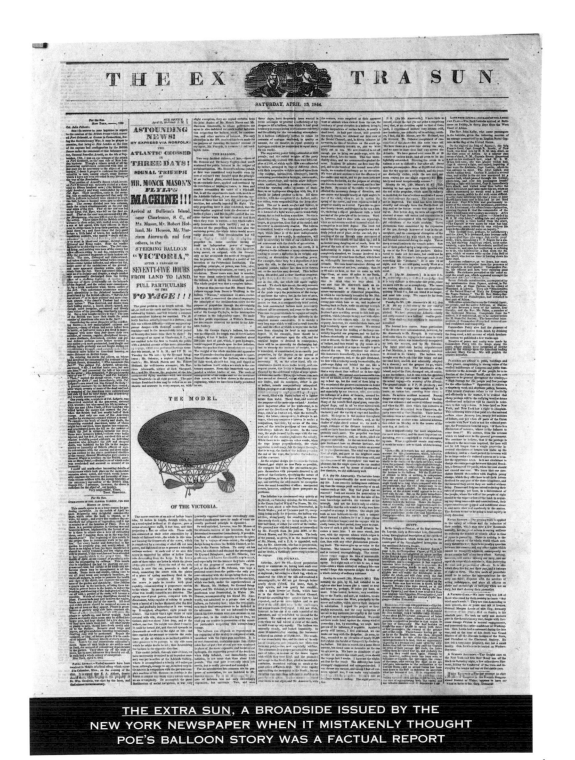

THE EXTRA SUN, A BROADSIDE ISSUED BY THE NEW YORK NEWSPAPER WHEN IT MISTAKENLY THOUGHT POE'S BALLOON STORY WAS A FACTUAL REPORT

Working for Willis must have been taxing, for Poe was expected to put in a fourteen-hour day. Add to that the time it took to walk to and from the office. Yet he kept writing and published several stories, and some poems. Soon after he arrived in New York he sold the New York *Sun* what is now known as "The Balloon Hoax." It appeared as the report of an actual crossing of the Atlantic Ocean in three days in a balloon. The New York *Sun,* terribly excited by what it took to be true, published a stop-press broadside headed ASTOUNDING NEWS! Some readers took it to be true, but the hoax was not a stunning success. Skeptical editors ridiculed the story and the author.

Still, it paid, if only a little. He ground out three gruesome comic stories laughing at the belief that technological progress would improve humanity. Even in such light pieces, Poe managed at times to work in references to dead-alive people and to father-versus-son situations.

Auguste Dupin, the detective, returned in two stories Poe wrote around this time—"The Purloined Letter" and "Thou Art the Man." In both stories Poe introduced new elements that authors of detective fiction would make use of: postmortem examinations, ballistic evidence, and the frame-up.

Even with steady work and a pleasant place to live, Poe found his spirits sagging. In October 1844 he wrote a friend that "I have reached a crisis in my life." One who dropped in on him at the *Mirror* office found him "very dejected." Where was his career going? Almost thirty-six, he was still scrabbling for the most meager living, doing dull work just to keep his family alive. And with all the stuff he poured out in the first year in the city, it brought in only about $450. Yet Americans expected you to be optimistic about life in this great country. In America? Poe asked, "where more than in any other region upon the face of the globe to be poor is to be despised?"

12

"The Raven"—and Fame

LUCK TURNED FOR POE WHEN IN DECEMBER 1844, Lowell recommended him for a job on the new literary magazine with a strong focus on cultural life, called the *Broadway Journal.* The editor was Charles F. Briggs, a Nantucket man who had been a sailor and had written an adventure novel that had made a great splash. Like Lowell, he was an abolitionist. In January, Poe was taken on as assistant editor, and soon promoted to coeditor. His assignment was to oversee the magazine in general and to write one page of his own each week. In return, he would be paid one-third of the magazine's profits at the end of each month. If he was not exactly an owner, neither was he a salaried hack.

The magazine published book reviews, criticisms of productions in art, theater, and music, as well as poetry and political essays. Poe checked in at the office at 9 A.M. and put in fourteen hours or more a day. "I never knew what it was to be a slave before," he said. He worked steadily and quietly with the staff. Briggs got to like Poe "exceedingly well," and hoped his reputation as a critic would bring in the book advertising the magazine depended on. Poe wrote appreciative pieces on many writers—Shelley, Milton, Tennyson, Lowell.

When it came to mediocre works, however, he was just as harsh as ever, especially if he thought writers had been treated too kindly and overpraised. He liked to say he "scalped" such authors, and asserted, "Feeble puffing is not my forte. It will do these fellows good to hear the truth and stimulate them to worthier efforts."

As he had on other editorial jobs, he made the mistake sometimes of being rude or arrogant with contributors to the *Journal,* needlessly creating enemies who might get even later. One of the worst examples occurred in his lecture on poetry February 28 at the New York Society Library. Years earlier Poe had hailed Longfellow for his "genius" and called him

"unquestionably the best poet in America." And Longfellow had responded with high praise of Poe. But now Poe accused Longfellow of plagiarizing one of his poems from a poem by Tennyson, when all they had in common was the theme. Longfellow never replied to these false charges. Later, after Poe's death, he would generously praise "his powers as a prose-writer and a poet."

Still writing for other publications, Poe gave *The Evening Mirror* a poem that would become one of the most famous ever written. It was "The Raven."

CHARLES F. BRIGGS, FOR WHOM POE WORKED ON THE BROADWAY JOURNAL

It appeared in the January 29, 1845, issue, running in a single column almost the full length of the back page. Willis, the editor, called it "unsurpassed in English poetry for subtle conception, masterly ingenuity of versification, and consistent, sustaining of imaginative lift . . . It will stick to the memory of everybody who reads it."

In writing it, Poe wanted to create a poem appealing to both the popular and the critical taste. The poem is the tale of a student grieving over the death of his beloved Lenore, when he is visited on a stormy night by an ominous bird, the raven. The student struggles to get over his obsession with his loss, and his loneliness, and to keep from going insane. Surely Virginia's worsening sickness and his fear of her death are reflected in the poem, and perhaps the never-absent memory of his mother's early passing.

The symbolic raven makes us recall other literary birds that figure in the Romantic tradition. There is the nightingale of John Keats, the skylark of Percy Bysshe Shelley, and the albatross of Samuel Taylor Coleridge. And in *Barnaby Rudge,* the Dickens novel Poe reviewed, there is Grip, the raven.

Response to the poem was overwhelming. You can't think of a superlative that editors and critics of that day didn't apply to it. Within a few weeks it was reprinted ten times. The extraordinary effects Poe created with sound made it a great choice for reading aloud. He took the poem on tour, thrilling audiences with his passionate reading. "The Raven" was soon adopted in textbooks on elocution or public speaking, and today is still recited in classrooms. (For any student trying to write poetry, Poe's own account of how "The Raven" was written is worth looking up. It was a passage in his essay on "The Philosophy of Composition." It can be found today in Harold Bloom's *Edgar Allan Poe,* Chelsea House, 1999.)

The smashing success of "The Raven" and Poe's prominence as editor of the *Broadway Journal* opened doors to New York's fashionable literary salons. Women especially were drawn to this poet not only for his genius and his influence in the literary world but for his notorious reputation. They liked to think they could reform or redeem him, rescue him from the harm done by his eccentric, even abnormal behavior.

Margaret Fuller, the brilliant New England author working for Horace Greeley's *New York Daily Tribune,* met Poe in these years. She said he was an isolated man who liked to imitate Lord Byron's tragic pose. "Several women loved him," she wrote, "but it seemed more with a passionate illusion, which he amused himself by inducing, than with sympathy . . . I think he really had no friends . . . He always seemed to me to be shrouded in an assumed character."

Among the women attracted to Poe were two who wrote poetry, though not of high quality. One was Frances "Fanny" Sargent Osgood, a charming woman Virginia liked so much she thought Fanny could help keep Poe from drinking. Fanny and Poe exchanged little poems written for each other. (He would use the same poem, maybe revised just a bit, to win the sympathy of several women.)

Another woman Poe met now and with whom he'd become intensely involved with later, was Sarah Helen Whitman, whose poetry he praised in his lecture on poetry.

In the summer of 1845, Poe saw an old friend, a wealthy southerner from

FRANCES SARGENT OSGOOD

Georgia, Dr. Thomas Holley Chivers. Chivers, who owned many slaves, had come to New York to seek publication of a volume of his poems. He visited Poe at the family's lodging on East Broadway, but Poe was so sick in bed, he could see no one. Virginia's condition struck Chivers as terribly serious. She was seized with coughing fits while he talked with her, so convulsive that they seemed "almost to rend asunder her very body."

The two men had something in common besides their identification with the South. Chivers's poems too brought in coffins, shrouds, angels, and reunions with the dead. Chivers in a memoir left this impression of Poe:

> His face was rather oval—tapering in the contour rather suddenly to the chin, which was very classical—and, especially when he smiled, really handsome . . . The form was slender, and by no means prepossessing—and appeared to me, in walking, to lean a little forward with a kind of meditative or Grecian bend . . . One of the most striking peculiarities of Mr. Poe was, his perfect abandon—boyish indifference—not only in regard to the opinions of others, but an uncompromising independence of spirit, which seemed to say he was oblivious to the prejudices of everybody . . . Yet no man living loved the praises of others better than he did.

In late November, Poe printed a piece on music education contributed by the young journalist and poet Walt Whitman. The two met in the offices of the *Broadway Journal.* Whitman recalled Poe as "dark, quiet, handsome—Southern from top to toe: languid, tired out . . . but altogether ingratiating." Later he would praise Poe for his "intense faculty for technical and abstract beauty [but] with the rhyming art to excess." Whitman, by then, had long given up on the "rhyming art."

The Raven

Once upon a midnight dreary, while I pondered, weak and weary
Over many a quaint and curious volume of forgotten lore,
While I nodded, nearly napping, suddenly there came a tapping,
As of some one gently rapping, rapping at my chamber door.
"'Tis some visitor," I muttered, "tapping at my chamber door—
    Only this and nothing more."

Ah, distinctly I remember it was in the bleak December;
And each separate dying ember wrought its ghost upon the floor.
Eagerly I wished the morrow;—vainly I had sought to borrow
From my books surcease of sorrow—sorrow for the lost Lenore—
For the rare and radiant maiden whom the angels name Lenore—
    Nameless here for evermore.

And the silken sad uncertain rustling of each purple curtain
Thrilled me—filled me with fantastic terrors never felt before;
So that now, to still the beating of my heart, I stood repeating,
"'Tis some visitor entreating entrance at my chamber door—
Some late visitor entreating entrance at my chamber door;—
    This it is and nothing more."

Presently my soul grew stronger; hesitating then no longer,
"Sir," said I, "or Madam, truly your forgiveness I implore;
But the fact is I was napping, and so gently you came rapping,
And so faintly you came tapping, tapping at my chamber door,
That I scarce was sure I heard you"—here I opened the door;—
    Darkness there and nothing more.

Deep into that darkness peering, long I stood there wondering,
  fearing,
Doubting, dreaming dreams no mortal ever dared to dream before;

LE CORBEAU

(THE RAVEN)

Poème d'Edgar POE

TRADUIT PAR STÉPHANE MALLARMÉ

Illustré de cinq Dessins de MANET

TEXTE ANGLAIS ET FRANÇAIS

Illustrations sur Hollande ou sur Chine

AU CHOIX

Couverture et Ex-Libris en parchemin. — Tirage limité.

PRIX : **25** FRANCS.

POE'S POPULARITY IN FRANCE WAS GREATER THAN AT HOME. THIS IS THE COVER OF THE FIRST FRENCH EDITION OF "THE RAVEN," TRANSLATED BY MALLARMÉ, A LEADING POET, WITH DESIGN BY MANET, A LEADING ARTIST.

But the silence was unbroken, and the stillness gave no token,
And the only word there spoken was the whispered word, "Lenore!"
This I whispered, and an echo murmured back the word "Lenore!"
 Merely this and nothing more.

Back into the chamber turning, all my soul within me burning,
Soon again I heard a tapping somewhat louder than before,
"Surely," said I, "surely that is something at my window lattice;
Let me see, then, what thereat [sic] is, and this mystery explore—
Let my heart be still a moment and this mystery explore;—
 'Tis the wind and nothing more!"

Open here I flung the shutter, when, with many a flirt and flutter,
In there stepped a stately raven of the saintly days of yore;
Not the least obeisance made he; not a minute stopped or stayed he;
But, with mien of lord or lady, perched above my chamber door—
Perched upon a bust of Pallas just above my chamber door—
 Perched, and sat, and nothing more.

Then this ebony bird beguiling my sad fancy into smiling,
By the grave and stern decorum of the countenance it wore,
"Though thy crest be shorn and shaven, thou," I said, "are sure no
 craven,
Ghastly grim and ancient raven wandering from the Nightly
 shore—
Tell me what thy lordly name is on the Night's Plutonian shore!"
 Quoth the Raven, "Nevermore."

Much I marvelled this ungainly fowl to hear discourse so plainly,
Though its answer little meaning—little relevancy bore;
For we cannot help agreeing that no sublunary being
Ever yet was blessed with seeing bird above his chamber door—
Bird or beast upon the sculptured bust above his chamber door,
 With such name as "Nevermore."

But the raven, sitting lonely on the placid bust, spoke only
That one word, as if his soul in that one word he did outpour.
Nothing farther then he uttered—not a feather then he fluttered—
Till I scarcely more than muttered, "Other friends have flown before—
On the morrow he will leave me, as my hopes have flown before."
     Then the bird said, "Nevermore."

Wondering at the stillness broken by reply so aptly spoken,
"Doubtless," said I, "what it utters is its only stock and store
Caught from some unhappy master whom unmerciful Disaster
Followed fast and followed faster so when Hope he would adjure—
Stern Despair returned, instead of the sweet Hope he dared adjure—
     That sad answer, 'Never—nevermore.'"

But the raven still beguiling my sad fancy into smiling,
Straight I wheeled a cushioned seat in front of bird, and bust and
   door;
Then, upon the velvet sinking, I betook myself to linking
Fancy unto fancy, thinking what this ominous bird of yore—
What this grim, ungainly, ghastly, gaunt and ominous bird of yore
     Meant in croaking "Nevermore."

This I sat engaged in guessing, but no syllable expressing
To the fowl whose fiery eyes now burned into my bosom's core;
This and more I sat divining, with my head at ease reclining
On the cushion's velvet lining that the lamp-light gloated o'er,
But whose violet velvet lining with the lamp-light gloating o'er,
     She shall press, ah, nevermore!

Then, methought, the air grew denser, perfumed from an unseen
   censer
Swung by Angels whose faint foot-falls tinkled on the tufted floor.
"Wretch," I cried, "thy God hath lent thee—by these angels he
   hath sent thee

Respite—respite and nepenthe from thy memories of Lenore;
Let me quaff this kind nepenthe and forget this lost Lenore!"
      Quoth the raven, "Nevermore."

"Prophet!" said I, "thing of evil!—prophet still, if bird or devil!
Whether Tempter sent, or whether tempest tossed thee here ashore,
Desolate yet all undaunted, on this desert land enchanted—
On this home by Horror haunted—tell me truly, I implore—
Is there—is there balm in Gilead?—tell me—tell me I implore!"
      Quoth the raven, "Nevermore."

"Prophet!" said I, "thing of evil—prophet still, if bird or devil!
By that Heaven that bends above us—by that God we both adore—
Tell this soul with sorrow laden if, within the distant Aidenn,
It shall clasp a sainted maiden whom the angels name Lenore—
Clasp a rare and radiant maiden whom the angels name Lenore."
      Quoth the raven, "Nevermore."

"Be that word our sign of parting, bird or fiend!" I shrieked,
    upstarting—
"Get thee back into the tempest and the Night's Plutonian shore!
Leave no black plume as a token of that lie thy soul hath spoken!
Leave my loneliness unbroken!—quit the bust above my door!
Take thy beak from out my heart, and take thy form from off my
    door!"
      Quoth the raven, "Nevermore."

And the raven, never flitting, still is sitting, still is sitting
On the pallid bust of Pallas just above my chamber door;
And his eyes have all the seeming of a demon that is dreaming,
And the lamp-light o'er him streaming throws his shadow on the
    floor;
And my soul from out that shadow that lies floating on the floor
    Shall be lifted—nevermore!

13

Death of the Beloved

ALTHOUGH POE WAS CHEERED WITH THE great run of "The Raven," it made him no money. "I am as poor now as ever I was in my life," he wrote, "except in hope, which is by no means bankable." It got even worse, for the *Broadway Journal* proved so unprofitable it folded by January 1846. A collection of Poe's *Tales* published in 1845 drew good reviews, in America and in Europe, yet earned only $120. And when another book, *The Raven and Other Poems*, appeared in the same year, he made little or nothing from it.

With income so uncertain, and Virginia's illness growing ever worse, Poe resumed drinking again. In between binges he told a friend, "I really believe that I have been mad." From this time on his literary creativity faded. He would reprint old stories and old poems rather than write new ones. He spent more time sniping at other writers than in building his own reputation. On one occasion, accepting an invitation to lead off with a new poem a literary series at the Boston Lyceum, he found himself unable to compose it. He could have withdrawn, but he needed the $50 fee. Instead of withdrawing he tried to palm off an old work, "Al Aaraaf," as a new one, giving it a different title. The audience thought him pathetic, and several walked out on him.

In May 1846, Poe moved his family out of the city. New York had become so crowded and dirty he feared it would worsen the ravages of Virginia's tuberculosis. He found a small frame house atop a hill in a rural area about 13 miles (20 kilometers) north of the city, in the village of Fordham (now part of the Bronx). For the cottage, built about 1812 as a laborer's dwelling, Poe paid an annual rent of $100. There were three small rooms on the ground floor, and two in the attic, one of which was Poe's study. A railroad extension had recently connected the village to the city. Nearby was St. John's College, where Poe found companionship among the

THE POE COTTAGE IN NEW YORK, IN THE FORDHAM NEIGHBORHOOD

Jesuit teachers. Often, when he was penniless, kindly neighbors fed the family.

As their first summer in the cottage wore on, Poe felt sick and so depressed he could not tackle any major work. Instead, he produced thirty-eight sketches for the Philadelphia magazine *Godey's Lady's Book.* They were his notes on "The Literati of New York City," often spiteful, for which he was paid $5 a column. His offensive comments on the appearance or manners of the writers he discussed and the venomous gossip he peddled created an uproar in literary circles while they tempted readers to buy up every copy of *Godey's.*

His aim was to rid New York of the curse of amateur authors, those privileged gentlemen who praised one another lavishly in publications they controlled. His light artillery opened up a full-scale war. He was accused in print of lying, of drunkeness, of insanity, of cowardice. He sued the owners of a New York newspaper for publishing libelous statements about him. He won, but it did nothing to regain his place in literary circles. I feel, he said, that I am being "driven to the very gates of death, and with a despair more dreadful than death." He thought of expanding the "Literati" pieces into a book assessing American literature, showing how social position determined a writer's success, how southern and western writers were rejected out of sectional hostility, and how writers were victimized by the lack of a copyright law. He fussed with this project for the next three years but never carried it out.

The family was so hard up that poet and newspaper editor William Cullen Bryant was approached by Mrs. Clemm. She asked him for money, saying "her son-in-law is crazy, his wife dying, and the whole family starving." At times she scoured the fields for edible herbs to feed the family.

In October, *Godey's* published "The Cask of Amontillado," the first tale Poe had written in a year. It deals with the passion for revenge, for telling a story as a means of getting even with all who have persecuted you. It echoes Poe's old theme, the inability to forget the past.

In this same season, as Poe's reputation and honor were challenged at home, his prestige was given a great boost abroad. One of the leading French literary journals published a twenty-page article on his work, discussing its importance in the development of fiction. Other periodicals in Paris carried translations of some of his stories, and in Russia, his "Gold Bug" appeared in translation.

As Virginia lay dying in the closing months of the year, a friend came by and found Poe "lost in a stupor, not living or suffering, but existing merely." Virginia was lying on white sheets covering a straw mattress, with Poe's old military over-coat covering her body, shivering with the alternating chills and fever of last-stage tuberculosis. Her mother, now fifty-six, had long ago lost her other two children, and her anguish over Virginia's approaching death and the family's poverty was "too dreadful to see," said a visitor.

In December, a New York paper reported that Poe and his wife were both "dangerously ill . . . and so far reduced as to be barely able to obtain the necessaries of life." The editor appealed to Poe's friends and readers to come to their aid. Other papers repeated deep concern, one crying out, "Great God! Is it possible that the literary people of the Union will let poor Poe perish by starvation and lean-faced beggary in New York?"

Poe's friend, the editor N. P. Willis, who had recently lost his own wife in childbirth, published an editorial in his magazine asking aid for Poe, "one of the finest scholars, one of the most original men of genius." The various appeals brought in several small contributions. Poe was warmed by the sympathy expressed, but the public attention to him as a charity case troubled him. Willis printed a letter from Poe saying he was down but not defeated, that he still had work to do, and would not give up till it was done.

Several friends came to offer help. It was Marie Louise Shew, twenty-five, who did the most for Virginia and for Poe, nursing both. Her father was a country doctor, and she grew up with deep sympathy for the poor and needy. Besides her nursing skills, she brought money raised from friends and her own warm comforter for Virginia. While she was nursing Virginia in the spring of 1846, Poe complained he was suffering from writer's block, and that bells ringing in the street kept disturbing him.

Marie suggested he write a poem about the bells and improvised an opening line to get him started. He responded, and created four stanzas, each describing a different kind of bell—sleigh bells, wedding bells, fire-alarm bells, funeral bells. The stanzas represented four phases of life—courtship, marriage, crisis, and mourning.

The Bells

(Opening Stanza)
Hear the sledges with the bells—
Silver bells!
What a world of merriment their melody foretells!
How they tinkle, tinkle, tinkle,
In the icy air of night!
While the stars that oversprinkle
All the heavens, seem to twinkle
With a crystalline delight;
Keeping time, time, time,
In a sort of Runic rhyme,
To the tintinnabulation that so musically wells
From the bells, bells, bells, bells,
Bells, bells, bells—
From the jingling and the tinkling of the bells.

"The Bells" is one of Poe's many experiments with the sound effects of language. He once said the primary principle of music is "the perception of pleasure in the equality of sounds." And this he applied to poetry. He manipulates words to suggest values beyond their usual meanings. Each stanza is longer than the one before it, with the last the longest, as the suffering of grief seems to have no end. It is one example of the musical elements of verse that Poe insisted on. He wants to suggest, not tell. For poetry is about what cannot be named. He worked on "The Bells" for more than a year. A Philadelphia magazine bought "The Bells," paying him $15. Over many generations it has been used as a recitation piece for boys and girls in school.

Their cat, who sat on Poe's shoulder when he worked, would rest on Virginia's bosom, helping to keep her warm, as her husband held her hands, and her mother her feet. Virginia's end did not come easily. She was unable to speak, except through her beautiful eyes. In her last night she suffered much pain. On Saturday, January 30, 1847, Poe's wife died. She was twenty-four, dying at the same age and of the same disease that had taken his mother and his brother.

The death of Virginia quickened Poe's own illness. A chronic fever that had weakened him for some time grew worse. Marie Shew, who had nursed his wife, and Poe too in his bad periods, thought his

THE BELLS.

———

I.

Hear the sledges with the bells—
Silver bells!
What a world of merriment their melody foretells!
How they tinkle, tinkle, tinkle,
In the icy air of night!
While the stars that oversprinkle
All the heavens, seem to twinkle

D

THE OPENING PAGE OF A LONDON EDITION OF "THE BELLS"

irregular heartbeat was due to a "lesion of the brain," not a cardiac condition. She knew that his drinking could turn him into a madman. She decided that because of the lesion of the brain he could not take the stimulant of liquor without its producing a kind of insanity, extreme suffering of the mind and body. Her observations conform with what others had observed of Poe's reaction when he took even one drink.

For many months after Virginia's death, Poe could not pull himself out of a deep depression. "The loss of his wife was a sad blow to him," a friend noted. "He did not seem to care, after she was gone, whether he lived an hour, a day, a week or a year; she was his all." While she had wavered between life and death it had driven him close to insanity, and trying to avoid collapse, he drank when he thought Virginia's mother would not know. My wife's death, he said, "I can and do endure as becomes a man." With the horrible oscillating between hope and despair now ended, he meant to go on with his life.

14

The Last Years

VIRGINIA WAS BURIED IN THE GRAVEYARD OF
the Dutch Reformed Church nearby. Marie Shew had bought
her coffin and her grave clothes. Often unable to sleep, Poe
took solitary walks that ended at Virginia's grave. In "Ulalume:
A Ballad," the only composition of this year, he used dramatic
and scenic effects to express his mourning. The rhythmic musical sounds echo wailing and lamentation. The poem ends with
a visit to the grave of the poet's beloved. It was not published
until December 1847.

With the settlement of his libel suit against the newspaper,
Poe received $225. He used it to buy new furnishings for the
cottage, wishing to make it more comfortable for Mrs. Clemm,
to whom he owed so much for her unfailing support. He
needed women's sympathy now more than ever. He looked for
it wherever he could.

This was a time in America, and in Europe, when great
changes were occurring, upheavals in the lives of millions. Yet
Poe, partly because of his grieving, and partly for his general
indifference to the world of social and economic change, took
little account of it in his writings.

POE IN 1848, THE YEAR BEFORE HIS DEATH

The war with Mexico, beginning in 1846, ended early in 1848 with a treaty by which the United States acquired 850,000 square miles (2,210,000 square kilometers), or about one-third of Mexico's land. It was more than the combined areas of France, Spain, and Italy. How would the new territories be organized? Would they be free or slave? Politics was in turmoil as a Free-Soil Party was formed to oppose slavery in the new territories.

In January 1848 gold was discovered in California. Men went crazy overnight as the news penetrated every corner of the country. A gold rush started one of the greatest mass migrations in history. While billions of dollars in gold were uncovered, it was at a terrible cost. Men returned to a brutal level of life—ruthless, reckless, driven by an elemental greed for riches. The values of common decency and caring for one another gave way to the habit of exploitation. Moneymaking became a mania.

In Europe that same year, revolutions broke out in country after country—France, Austria, Germany, Italy, Hungary, Denmark. Poe always had something to say about literary quarrels, often those he provoked, but little about events that shook the lives of so many. Instead, he concentrated on writing a long book of prose, a philosophical treatise, completed in 1848. The theme was vague, mystical—man's relation to God and the universe.

Neglecting to get his facts straight, Poe grappled with scientific theories about the origin and nature of the universe. In trying to fit his superficial knowledge into a philosophical system he confidently predicted he would "revolutionize the world" of science and philosophy.

In February 1848, Poe tried out his new work before a New York audience. He expected to draw several hundred, but only about sixty showed up. He talked for two and a half hours. His listeners had varied responses. Some thought the talk profound or imaginative but not persuasive, while another termed it a "mountainous piece of absurdity for a popular lecture."

A few months later Poe had worked the lecture up into a book of about 150 pages. He called it *Eureka: A Prose Poem*. Putnam's published it in 500 copies, at 75 cents. It sold poorly. It would be the longest and the last of his ten books to be published. One critic dismissed it as "little more than elementary school stuff, dressed up in highfalutin language." Another said its value is "absolutely nil." And a third called it "a rambling, incoherent and excruciatingly boring book." One reviewer said the book was a mishmash of "astronomical systems, concentric circles, centrifugal forces, planetary distance, the Nebular theory and the star Alpha Lyrae."

When the book was finished, Poe began drinking again. A young theological student who had gotten to know him at Fordham, hearing that he was missing, found him "crazy-drunk in the hands of the police" and took him back to the cottage. When the student saw how empty the kitchen shelves were, he left $5. Marie Shew, who had nursed Virginia in the last days, and was so warm a friend and helper, now saw that he was drinking madly. She could not put up with it any longer. You won't live long, she told him, unless you find a woman tough enough and tender enough to give you the care you desperately need.

She was right; Poe knew it. He set about trying to find that woman. His last year of life was a wild whirlwind of approaches to four different women. There is little point in going into detail on these brief affairs. Nothing but grief came of any of them. His deep despair, his bouts of drunkenness, and what may have been the signs of insanity, drove women away.

He managed somehow to pursue subscribers to the *Stylus*, supporting himself by lecturing on "The Poetic Principle" in cities both North and South. That lecture voiced his views on "the mythic creation of beauty." Pleasure, not instruction, he insisted, is the aim of poetry. The reviews the series drew were excellent. One paper called the lecture "one of the richest intellectual treats we have ever had the good fortune to hear." In this lecture as well as in earlier essays, twentieth-century scholars held, Poe "erected the foundation of serious criticism in America." Though emotionally fragile, he could still create at the highest level.

But he was paranoid at times, convinced that some men were plotting to kill him. Now and then he would collapse into unconsciousness, and hallucinate wildly.

Yet his lectures didn't go off badly, although people remarked how pale and nervous he seemed to be. Arriving in Baltimore toward the end of September, he vanished for five days. It was the eve of a local election in a town notoriously corrupt. Later a dubious story spread that he had fallen into the hands of a political gang and held in a drugged or drunken condition, as they carried him from poll to poll, using him as a repeater-voter.

On election day he was found strangely dressed and in a semi-conscious condition at a tavern by Joseph Walker, a printer. Poe told him to reach Dr. Joseph E. Snodgrass, an old friend. Snodgrass came and with help got Poe to a hospital, where he was placed in the care of Dr. J. J. Moran, a young resident physician. Poe was incoherent, delirious, raving for a day or more. Then, resting for a few moments, Moran reported, "he said 'Lord help my poor Soul,' and expired."

It was Sunday, October 7, 1849, at 5 in the morning, when Poe died. He was forty years old.

The precise cause of his death is unknown. Medical experts have speculated about what might have led to his death: alcoholic poisoning, brain fever, nervous prostration, cerebral epilepsy, apoplexy, rabies. It was most likely a combination of causes.

Dr. Moran made the funeral arrangements, with the help of Rev. W.D.T. Clemm, a Baltimore cousin of Virginia's. Poe was buried the day after his death, on Monday afternoon, October 8. About eight people came to the small Presbyterian cemetery, which held the graves of Henry Poe, Edgar's brother, and General David Poe, his grandfather. Under a cold and desolate sky, the ceremony took only a few minutes.

POE'S GRAVESTONE IN THE CEMETERY AT RICHMOND, VIRGINIA

That so few came to mourn the loss of Poe is due in part to the fact that news of his death began to appear in the press only the day after his burial. That was how Mrs. Clemm heard. She could hardly believe it, and said, "God have mercy on me, for he was the last I had to cling to and love." She received many letters of sympathy from literary figures, and a visit from Longfellow.

Acting innocently on her own, Mrs. Clemm gave Poe's archenemy, Rufus Griswold, the right to contract for a multi-volume edition of Poe's prose and poetry. It would be of no help to the poor bereaved woman, for the publisher gave her nothing but a few sets for her own use. Even worse was the obituary notice that Griswold wrote anonymously for the New York *Tribune,* and which other newspapers reprinted. He opened by asking in effect who would mourn for Poe? A man with few or no friends. He went on to smear Poe for a dozen different weaknesses and faults, depicting him as a skilled writer, yes, but a cynical and unprincipled man.

When other writers came publicly to Poe's defense, Griswold countered with a long preface he wrote for the final volume of his edition of Poe's works. It included many deliberate lies, and even passages attributed to Poe that Griswold made up, and calculated to make Poe appear to be some kind of monster.

Unfortunately, Griswold's treacherous inventions were taken as truth by many, and were often repeated in articles and books about Poe in the years to come. Not until 1880 did modern scholarship finally prevail, when a new biography exposed the lies and brought the true facts to light.

In his short and turbulent life Poe produced about one hundred poems and seventy stories. It is more than 160 years since his death, yet writers continue to find they can learn something from his art. And readers continue to be drawn to—and intrigued by—the haunting themes of Poe's poetry and prose.

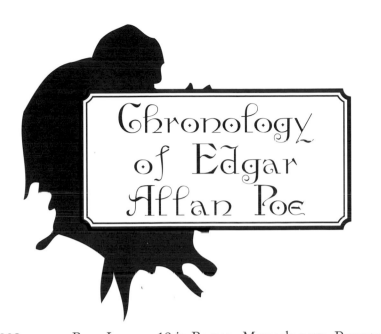

Chronology of Edgar Allan Poe

1809	Born January 19 in Boston, Massachusetts. Parents are actors Eliza Arnold Poe and David Poe.
1811	Father disappears. Mother dies December 8. Edgar becomes the ward of John and Frances Allan.
1815–1820	Moves with Allans to England. Attends boarding schools.
1820	Family returns to Richmond, Virginia. Poe attends local school.
1822	Composes early poems.
1825	Allan inherits wealth from uncle William Galt.
1826	Poe enters University of Virginia. Does well but incurs gambling debts.
1827	Drops out of college. Leaves Richmond for Boston. Publishes *Tamerlane and Other Poems.* Joins U.S. Army. Stationed at Fort Moultrie, South Carolina.
1829	Foster mother Frances Allan dies. Poe leaves army. Moves to Baltimore, begins writing fiction. Publishes *Al Aaraaf, Tamerlane, and Minor Poems.*
1830	Receives appointment to West Point Military Academy. Hires military replacement. Allan remarries and severs ties with Poe.

1831	Poe expelled from West Point. In New York, publishes *Poems.* Moves to Baltimore. Lives in poverty with his Aunt Maria Clemm and her daughter Virginia. His brother Henry dies August 1.
1832	Philadelphia magazine, the *Saturday Courier,* publishes five stories by Poe. Seeks work in Baltimore. John Allan writes will, excludes Poe.
1833	Lives with grandmother, aunt, and cousin. Writes satirical "Folio Club" tales. Wins Baltimore *Saturday Visiter* contest with a story.
1834	*Godey's Lady's Book* begins to publish Poe's work. John Allan dies, leaves Poe no inheritance. Poe family living in poverty in Baltimore.
1835	Leaves family to take editing job for *Southern Literary Messenger* in Richmond. In September, quits job and returns to aunt and cousin in Baltimore. Gets job with *Messenger* back and moves family to Richmond. Reviews many books, publishes several new tales.
1836	Marries cousin Virginia Clemm in May.
1837	Dismissed as editor of *Messenger.* Moves family to New York City. Publishes first two chapters of his only novel, *The Narrative of Arthur Gordon Pym*, in the *Messenger.* Harper agrees to take *Pym*, promising publication for following year.
1838	Moves to Philadelphia with wife and Aunt Maria Clemm. *Pym* published. Writes "Ligeia."
1839	Becomes coeditor of *Burton's Gentlemen's Magazine.* Publishes six installments of "The Journal of Julius Rodman" in *Burton's.* Publishes "The Man That Was Used Up" and "The Fall of the House of Usher" in *Burton's* and "William Wilson" in an annual gift book. His first twenty-five stories published in the volume *Tales of the Grotesque and Arabesque.* Begins cryptography series for *Alexander's Weekly Messenger.*
1840	Dismissed as editor of *Burton's.* Unable to find enough subscribers for his own journal, *The Penn Magazine.*

1841	Hired as an editor of *Graham's Magazine*, to which he contributes reviews and tales, including first detective story, "The Murders in the Rue Morgue." Seeks but fails to get government job.
1842	Virginia ill with tuberculosis. Poe drinks heavily. Meets Charles Dickens, resigns from *Graham's*. Seeks editorial work in New York. Publishes "The Masque of the Red Death," "The Mystery of Marie Rogêt," and "The Pit and the Pendulum."
1843	Revives plan for his own magazine, renamed the *Stylus*. Visits Washington in vain search for government job. Lectures on poetry. "The Gold Bug" wins prize from Philadelphia paper. Writes "The Tell-Tale Heart" and "The Black Cat."
1844	Moves with family back to New York City. Creates sensation with "The Balloon Hoax." Works for *The Evening Mirror*. Places eleven stories in various periodicals.
1845	Wins fame with "The Raven," published in January. Gives readings of it, but gains little money. Becomes coeditor of *The Broadway Journal*. Publishes new edition of *Tales* and *The Raven and Other Poems*.
1846	*Broadway Journal* closes. Boston Lyceum poetry reading causes uproar. Family moves to Fordham cottage. Writes "Literati of New York City" sketches for *Godey's*. Publishes "The Philosophy of Composition" and "The Cask of Amontillado." Writes "The Bells."
1847	Virginia dies of tuberculosis in January. Poe seriously ill. Wins libel lawsuit. Writes satires, parodies, poem "Ulalume."
1848	Revives *Stylus* project. Composes *Eureka*. Travels to lecture and solicit subscriptions. Courts several women.
1849	Continues traveling to lecture and secure subscriptions to *Stylus*. Disappears for a time, collapses in Baltimore, taken to hospital, dies on October 7.

Reading Poe Himself

Much of Poe's work was not published in book form in his lifetime. Almost all his poems and stories and essays were written for periodicals—newspapers and magazines. He wanted book publication above all else, and managed to get ten books into print, plus pamphlet editions of two stories.

Since his death, there have been a great many books with selections from his writings. In the following list are those I made use of, all of them easily available:

Edgar Allan Poe: Poems and Prose. New York: Everyman's Library, 1995.

Edgar Allan Poe: Tales of Terror and Detection. New York: Dover, 1995.

The Complete Poems of Edgar Allan Poe. New York: Barnes & Noble, 1999.

Kennedy, J. Gerald, ed. *Edgar Allan Poe: Arthur Gordon Pym and Related Tales.* New York: Oxford, 1998.

Levine, Stuart, and Susan F. Levine, eds. *Edgar Allan Poe: 32 Stories.* Indianapolis, IN: Hackett, 2000.

Visiting Edgar Allan Poe Sites

The Edgar Allan Poe Cottage, where he spent the last four years of his life, from 1846 to 1849, has been restored to its original appearance. Located at Kingsbridge Road and the Grand Concourse, Bronx, New York. Open all year for guided tours. Saturday 10 A.M.–4 P.M.; Sunday 1 P.M.–5 P.M. Tours during week by appointment. Call Bronx County Historical Society, 718-881-8900.

The Baltimore Poe House and Museum, 203 Amity Street in West Baltimore. Hours of operation:

    April–July: Wed.–Sat., Noon–3:45 P.M.
    August–September: Sat., Noon–3:45 P.M.
    October–December: Wed.–Sat., Noon–3:45 P.M.
    January–March: closed for season and repairs

There is a charge for admission.
Phone: 410-396-7932

The Edgar Allan Poe Museum, 1914-16 East Main Street, between 19th and 20th Streets, Richmond, Virginia. Hours are Tuesday through Saturday from 10 A.M. to 5 P.M., with guided tours beginning on the hour. For more information see http://www.poemuseum.org

Index

Page numbers in *italics* refer to illustrations.

About the Author

THE LIFE OF EDGAR ALLAN POE IS ANOTHER IN Meltzer's series of biographies of poets, following his *Langston Hughes, Walt Whitman,* and *Carl Sandburg.* He has written more than one hundred books for young people and adults.

Born in Worcester, Massachusetts, Meltzer was educated at Columbia University. He lives with his wife in New York City. They have two daughters and two grandsons.

In 2001 he received the Laura Ingalls Wilder award from the American Library Association for his "substantial and lasting contributions to literature for children." The year before, the Catholic Library Association awarded him the Regina Medal for his lifetime achievement. Five of his books have been finalists for the National Book Award. He has won the Carter G. Woodson, Christopher, Jane Addams, Jefferson Cup, Olive Branch, and Golden Kite awards. His titles frequently appear on the "best books of the year" lists of the American Library Association, the National Council for the Social Studies, the National Council of Teachers of English, and *The New York Times* Best Books of the Year lists.